ALIENS & ANOREXIA

CHRIS KRAUS

ALIENS & ANOREXIA

CHRIS KRAUS

All song lyrics in *Gravity & Grace*
copyright Barbara Barg/Homer Erotic.
Radio segments were written and
produced by John Kelsey.
Additional dialogue was co-written with
Ann Rower.

Portions of this book were reprinted in
Inflatable, *Log*, *Flesh-Eating Technologies*,
and *Issue*.

Smart Art Press Volume VII, No. 66

ISBN # 1–58435–001–6
Cover Design: Mick Haggerty
Type Design: Peter Kim and Tim Koh

Printed in the United States of America

Table of Contents

I am grateful to the following people for their insightful readings of this book at different stages: Sylvère Lotringer, Laurie Stone, Giovanni Intra, Ann Rower, Ochiishi Augustmoon, Leslie Mohn, Heather Lewis and Jim Fletcher; and to Susan Martin, Mark Stritzel, Ben Meyers, Jim Fleming, Peter Kim and Mick Haggerty for their patience and help with production. Thanks also to Richard Hertz for his continued encouragement of my work, and to the Faculty Advisory Council at Art Center for an Enrichment Grant that made it possible to travel.

Semiotext(e) gratefully acknowledges financial assistance in the publication of this book from the Literature Program of the New York State Council on the Arts

This book is dedicated to the memory of
David Rattray and Lily

Countdown on the millennium clock at 34th Street and 7th Avenue in Manhattan, a grid of twitching light-dots advancing into numbers, ringed by brightly-colored logos of its sponsors burned into the plastichrome – TCBY Yogurt, Roy Rogers, Staples and Kentucky Fried Chicken – a neo-medieval message from our sponsors, instructing us that time is fluid but Capital is here to stay –

468 days, 11 hours, 43 minutes, 16 seconds to go

1.

New York City, Autumn 1978:

IT IS a large room on the second floor where Pisti and Eva live. Squat Theater, a Hungarian group of actors-artists-underground intellectuals whose work was banned in Budapest because it was "morally offensive, obscene" and did not "serve the objectives of the government's cultural policy" are now living in a building on West 23rd Street, New York City with their children. They need a place where they can live and work, where they can dissolve and realign the boundaries between their collective daily life and their performances, the inside of their theater/house, the passersby and traffic in the street. They spend months planning and discussing the details of all of their performances, but they do not rehearse.

In *Andy Warhol's Last Love*, Eva Buchmiller, a young woman with long hair in a short black slip sits in front of a bookcase at a table. She is channeling the voice of the dead Ulrike Meinhof through a set of headphones. She is smoking while she listens very hard:

> ..... zzzzz ......
> *This is Ulrike Meinhof speaking to the inhabi-*
> *tants of Earth. You must make your death public.*
> *On the night of May 9th 1976 in a special iso-*
> *lation cell of the Stammheim Prison where I was*
> *confined without sentence by order of the Chief*
> *Prosecutor of the Federal Republic of Germany,*
> *as co-leader of the Red Army Fraction....*

zzzzzzzz

As the rope was tightening around my neck,
moment of losing my mind, suddenly I lost my
perception but regained all my consciousness
and discernment. An Alien made love with me.

If it is true as certain newspapers write, that
traces of sperm were found on my dress, these
could be the traces of intercourse.

After making love, I could state that my con-
sciousness went on functioning in a new and
uninjured body.

Afterward the Alien took me to a special planet
which belongs to Andromedas. The society
there treats time and space with intensity, gen-
tleness, discipline and freedom. Over...

In this play, Andy Warhol and Ulrike Meinhof, two
cultural icons who might seem literally to oppose each other,
come together – They are a dialectical synthesis transposed
to psychic states. Years later, Buchmiller wrote: "Ulrike
Meinhof is a legend who turned politics into tragic poetry...
According to the principles of pop culture, Andy Warhol is
a clone of himself. Thus, he is as real as he can get. How did
Andy Warhol meet with Ulrike Meinhof? By chance."

ON THE 17th of January in 1996, I traveled from Los Angeles to Berlin.

I was traveling to Germany to attend the Berlin Film Festival, or, to be more accurate, since *Gravity & Grace*, the low-budget independent film that I'd been producing, writing, directing, editing and now distributing for the past three years had already been rejected twice in all three categories of the Berlin Film Festival, I was traveling to Germany to attend the European Film Market. In recent years, the European Film Market had been attached commercially as a sidebar to the Festival – a profitable trade show in which product deemed unsuitable for the Festival is bought and sold. Hundreds of European television dramas, Asian action movies, Latin American thrillers change hands among producers and distributors, TV acquisition agents, entertainment lawyers, banks and government consortiums. The European Film Market is the best venue for the secondary market of "world" film, i.e., anything produced outside of Hollywood.

Gravity & Grace was an experimental 16mm film about hope, despair, religious feeling and conviction. Driven harder by philosophy than plot or character, it skirted round the edges of the lives of two teenage girls and a disillusioned woman in her 40s.

Diary entry on the plane from Los Angeles to London, January 17, first nine hours of the 20 hour trip: "*I don't want to go to Berlin.*"

Because none of my acquaintances or friends wanted to be the one to say the film had failed, they all pretended that this 'invitation' to attend the European Film Market was an honor and an opportunity. And then there was the urban myth that Jennifer Montgomery, the ex-girlfriend of my friend, the poet Eileen Myles, had signed a distribution deal last year at the Market for her feature film *The Teaching of Children* with New Yorker Films *even though* the film had been rejected by the Festival...

But *Gravity & Grace* was just so unappealing. It was an amateur intellectual's home video expanded to bulimic lengths, shot and edited between three countries with a cast and crew of 70 or 80, costing about the price of a two-bedroom Park Slope co-op. In the six months following its completion, the film had been rejected by every major festival from Sundance to Australia to Turin.

Luckily, the New York Foundation for the Arts ran a program to service movies just like these. Started by the enterprising Lynda Hansen, the American Independents delegation bought out a block of slots each year at the European Film Market and resold them to a dozen filmmakers. The price – about $3000 – paid for market registration and a single screening of the film. NYFA offered as a bonus, *free of charge*, inclusion of a one-page guff sheet for each movie in their American Independents promotional brochure and access at the Market to "the Booth," which amounted to a message pigeonhole for each producer, which, as it turned out in my case, no one used.

By January 1996 I'd been living out of suitcases for two and a half years, raising money, hustling money, pimping the services of my husband, a distinguished European intellectual, to finance the film. Once, I thought I'd hit a high point of surrender to the movie's waste, spending $350 on a single Fed-Ex, shipping 16 mm A&B rolls from New Zealand when the promise of free laboratory processing fell through, to

Toronto where at least the rate of change was low. And yet I sensed I wasn't at the end yet. There is a symmetry in following a spiral down as far as it will go. In LA, my friend Pam Strugar helped me make a bunch of home-made press kits – I remember a discussion about what color paperclips to use – and so I wrote a check to NYFA, bought a plane ticket and went.

Because the 35 pound answerprint of *Gravity & Grace* was practically irreplaceable, I was carrying it, together with a bag of presskits, on the plane. And this worked out well, because the airline lost my bags at Heathrow while I was waiting to catch the plane to Berlin-Tegel that'd been postponed. It took three days to find them.

After 24 hours of travel, I stepped out into the cold and leaden air of January with the movie and no winter clothes. I was carrying a piece of paper with the address and phone number of the woman I was to stay with, who was a sometime friend of a public radio producer in Los Angeles I barely knew. Gudrun Scheidecker was expecting me; we'd talked once on the phone. She'd once stayed a month one summer with the radio producer, who inexplicably saw my visit to the Market as an opportunity to extract repayment for some kind of debt, and I'd leapt at these arrangements because the rate of change between the US dollar and the German mark was low. By that time, I knew all about the rates of foreign currencies.

So in the early evening of January 18, wearing nothing but a sweater over traveling clothes, carrying the print and press kits, I took a taxi from the airport to Gudrun Scheidecker's apartment in a central suburb known as Kleistpark.

Because both of us were girls, Gudrun Scheidecker told

me everything about her life.

Although, as she herself quickly pointed out, she looked much younger, Gudrun Scheidecker was 48 years old. She'd never married but she had two lovers whose existences she'd been hiding from each other. This sounded complex but it ran according to a timetable: the first, she saw on Mondays and Thursdays; the second, Saturdays and Wednesdays and on the remaining nights she slept alone.

In Europe, certain kinds of counter-cultural time stand still. Gudrun Scheidecker spoke several European languages and described herself as a high-school teacher and a traveler. Her job allowed for unpaid leaves of absences, so she worked just long enough to stop and travel for a year. The city of Berlin wasn't trying hard enough to flush the Gudrun Scheideckers out of upscale Kleistpark: she boasted that she'd had this unheated two-room rent controlled apartment with high ceilings for some thirty years.

Suddenly, Gudrun Scheidecker flashed her well-kept unstyled long brown hair and asked me if I liked the artist Sophie Calle. "Um, I guess," I said. "I *love* her," Gudrun squealed, "because she's just like me!" And then she told me all about the new "hobby" she'd been pursuing to console herself during the years she couldn't be in Bali or Sumatra or Fiji: "Do you remember the project Sophie made with the address book? Well," she said, "sometimes I like to walk around the streets and look for good-looking men. I test for how long I can follow them without them seeing me."

I looked at her with horror: a lanky woman wearing boots and jeans, a hand-knit sweater, the full dark lips and creamy skin of someone 28 years old. At 50, Gudrun Scheidecker had no past and no attachments, no profession, no possessions, nothing but her youthful looks to show. Curiously, the spectacle of Gudrun made me feel quite young. When you're young, you look at older women like they're ciphers. Ciphers that you'd rather not decode, because you know you might be looking at your future. Their defeats and compromises are so visible. You wonder if they notice that you're studying their faces as they speak: the sagging flesh around their mouths and foreheads, the heavy fragile eyelids, wondering *could she be me?* Vague apprehension of a girl believing that she'll beat the odds, although she knows full well the woman that she sees was also once a girl... Not wanting, then, to think too much about how anybody gets from here to there; or more precisely, not wanting to imagine the events that might deform a person over twenty years...

By that time it was dark and snowing. Gudrun Scheidecker helped me put my things away. Inside the apartment, it was cold. The room that we'd been sitting in, Gudrun's bedroom, was heated with a small ceramic stove she stoked with coal. She gave me two wool blankets as she said goodnight because the second room, the guest room, had no heat at all.

The next morning, Gudrun handed me a subway map and wished me well. It was Monday morning. I caught the U-Bahn to the junction of the Kudaam, opposite the Zoo. A huge marquee outside the headquarters of the Berlin Film Festival announced the world premiere, tomorrow night, of an action movie starring Sharon Stone. The European Film Market was housed in a nearby office building that had been transformed this week into a convention center with four floors, six screening rooms, 340 information booths and 6,000 hungry media professionals.

The American Independents Delegation booth was located in a back corner near the Kodak Film display on the third floor. Gordon Laird, the New York Foundation for the Arts coordinator of this "delegation," who I'd never met but talked to on the phone, handed me an information pack and schedule, then turned to greet someone important.

Well, I had nowhere else to go, nothing to do, so I leaned against the booth and looked through the brochures. Inside there was a list of screening times for the delegation's dozen movies. Already I was sensing timing was important, there were a thousand screenings, and *Gravity & Grace* was scheduled to screen at 9 a.m. on Friday, the last day of the Market. I imagined people stumbling into the convention hall around 11, if at all, after a raucous closing party, or maybe several, which I also noticed I was not invited to. And everybody knows, the parties are the most important thing of all. The only way I'd gotten any meetings in Rotterdam at the Cinemarket two years before had been by getting drunk and flirting with an ex-philosopher turned producer by telling him I was the grand-niece of the satirist Karl Kraus. And yet the only party invitation here was for a single NYFA-sponsored cocktail party Tuesday night…

I tugged on Gordon's sleeve and asked him, "What about the parties?" "Don't worry," he replied, "you'll meet people who'll invite you to the other parties."

Already this was seeming doubtful. All around us, business was in full swing and I was sweating, with no place to put the heavy shearling coat that Gudrun'd loaned me 'til my bags arrived, and so I shrugged and cracked a charmingly self-deprecating smile. "Well, Gordon, I guess if nothing else I'll get to see a lot of movies." He looked quizzically at me.

"This is a market. Screenings are open only to the buyers."
Instantly my mind flashed upon the triangle between the
convention center, the Kleistpark U-Bahn Station, and
Gudrun Scheidecker's apartment. I had no contacts, no
appointments. "Remember now, you're here to network,"
Gordon said, dismissing me.

"Wait!" I said. No matter how much Gordon Laird hated
me, how insignificant, absurd my presence was, I was a New
York Jew, entitled to seek value for my money. "About my
screening – it's so early, on the last day of the Market, do you
really think that anyone will come?" Gordon looked at me
and said: "That all depends on you. You know, you have to
work the Market, hand out flyers."

My face flashed forward to a picture of myself, leafleting
the Market floor in Gudrun's shearling coat like a Jehovah's
Witness. It was not a pleasant image. Gordon caught it. "You
know," he said, "it might be possible for you to buy a second
screening at a better time."

When I agreed, he turned me over to his assistant Pam,
a young Black woman out of Sarah Lawrence College who
gave me forms to fill and told me who to see. This project
occupied another forty minutes and cost $300. And after all
of that, it was still just 11:30 in the morning. Business was
being transacted all around in other languages, and there was
no place to sit down without paying $3 for a coffee and even
if I did, no one would talk to me.

Outside it was gray and slushy. I shivered through the
coat that I'd been sweating in all morning. Standing on the
sidewalk with a big fat European Film Market Directory, a
portable office in my handbag, home-made press releases,
xeroxed letterhead, a felt tip pen, I'd reached the final

destination of the movie, thinking, *This is where it ends.*

WITHIN MOMENTS of her death in 1976, Ulrike Meinhof became an Alien. "It's only at the moment of death when an earthling can achieve the quality and intensity which Aliens start with." In the Squat Theater play, Andy Warhol arrives in the financial district of Manhattan riding a white horse. Meinhof comes back to meet him, inhabiting the host-body of a child. Zzzzzz. "You must," she says, "make your death public."

As channeled by Squat Theater, the myth of Warhol and the myth of Meinhof meet in a performance. Instead of scripting it, "a potential field of action was staked out." This unpredictability made reality alive, and much more immanently theatrical than theater.

Long before the artist Gerhard Richter physicalized her mythic image in his blurry spectral paintings, Meinhof had recast her life as myth. How did she become one? While Andy Warhol, as Squat Theater says, "turned exhausted art into daily food and gained freedom in complete unity with the existing world," Meinhof lived in opposition. Eva Buchmiller sees her politics existing outside of historical time, an act of "tragic poetry."

What moves me most about Meinhof's life is the way she underwent a public transformation. The way she left the conscious, conscience-driven world of academic public discourse far behind and entered, just before her death, a realm of pure sensation. As Squat describes an actor's job, so she lived, "manifesting an existence that overrode its representation."

Ulrike Meinhof crossed the line between activist and terrorist on May 14, 1970 when she helped Andreas Baader to escape from Tegel Prison. Posing as the TV journalist she often was, she set up an interview with him at the toney German Institute for Social Questions. When he arrived manacled between two prison guards she was waiting with her press card and a gun. Then two girls with wigs and briefcases walked in on cue and started flirting with the guards, creating a distraction for the masked man who entered brandishing a gun. In a blur that lasted thirty seconds, Ulrike pushed one the of wall-length leaded windows open, grabbed Andreas' hand and jumped. They hit the ground and ran.

Until that time, Meinhof had been an increasingly militant but highly visible journalist and intellectual. Married briefly to Klaus Rohl, a mainstream communist official who later claimed to have taught her everything she knew. "Her love for communism and for me," he wrote later in a self-serving biography, "amounted to the same thing." At 18 she was considered brilliant, winning scholarships and prizes, courted by the leadership of Rohl's own party who saw a great political career in Meinhof's future.

At 27, she was editor-in-chief of *Konkret*, an influential political magazine. She and Rohl had twin daughters and a country house. She lectured, commented on politics for television, wrote. She was the token woman on every panel. And yet, she didn't like her life. "The relationship with Klaus, the house, the parties, all that is only partially fun; it provides me with a basis... to be a subversive element... It is even pleasing personally, but does not fill my need for warmth, solidarity, for belonging to a group," she wrote in her diary when she was 31 years old.

During Meinhof's difficult pregnancy, which caused her ceaseless, blinding headaches, Rohl took over her editorship at *Konkret* and turned it into a kind of German *Evergreen*: politics mixed in with arty pix of naked hippie girls, "a jerk-off rag," she called it. In 1968 she divorced him and led a widely publicized insurrection at the magazine.

And then she took a year off and spent it researching a television play called *Bambule*. She hung around the Eichenhof, a reform school in Berlin for illiterate, fucked up teenage girls. Meinhof had achieved her influence and success because she was never at a loss for words, but at that moment she fell in love with the confused logic of their voices. She found herself unable to objectify them; fought with the director; rebelled against the journalist's role.

In the script published years after her death in 1976, Meinhof lets her subjects speak in the stark and blunted rhythm of their own words about what keeps them in the streets. She introduces the story of Irena from the observer's stance: "Irena's history was a fairy tale, a joke. She ended up with the police involved, locked in solitary confinement..." And then Irena's voice takes over...

Erica and me used to be allowed out into the courtyard. They were hoping that we'd break something. But we didn't give them that satisfaction. Instead we stayed downstairs and plotted. Erica looked outside and she saw the teacher was gone and she said she wanted to split – and she asked, Did we want to help her? And we said Yeah, sure. So Erica went and got a ladder and she put it up against the wall but she fell and nearly broke her neck. Well, we started cursing.

*So finally it was me who started. I climbed up onto the wall
and started stacking stones to jump from. And then Erica did it
too, she climbed the wall and started stacking stones, and as soon
as Erica made up her mind to do it, she was gone!*

*I went back downstairs and they said to me, What've you
been doing. And I said nothing. And they said Nothing? What
does that mean, Nothing? Where's Erica? What're those stones?
Well, I said. Then one word led to another word and finally I
owned up. And they asked if anyone else was involved, and I said
NO! IT WAS JUST ME!*

*Well, here we go again – solitary confinement. And then they
threatened to call the cops. Go ahead, I said, I don't give a shit.
Well I didn't think they'd really call the cops but they did and two
cops came, and one of them kicked me, and the other one tied my
hands behind my back and before you knew it, I was back in the
hole...*

And then Meinhof-the-journalist discovers the psychic
mobility of fiction. She flips. She empathizes, starts to speak
from the position of the girls:

*Girls end up in Eichenhof because there's no one to look after
them. To have no one: that means there's no bread and butter
waiting for you when you come home from work, you have to fix
it for yourself. And so you walk around the streets, you spend a
little money, you don't sleep at night, but above all it means
having no one to turn to except yourself.*

As a working journalist and intellectual, Meinhof felt a
certain empathy but had no direct emotional connection to
what frightened and seduced her most about these girls: the

absence of ambition, the lack of plans, the floating state of being lost and insignificant. Unlike her contemporary Alexander Kluge, who anthropologized the troubled teenager "Anita G." in his acclaimed movie *Yesterday's Girl*, Meinhof was willing to think about the distance that separated herself and her young subjects *as a subject*. Yet still, they were worlds apart.

Could Meinhof's entry into "armed struggle" really be a war of language? Direct action as escape from the self-conscious claustrophobia of arrogant, objectifying discourse. One year later she was friends with Gudrun Esselin, a member of the RAF, masterminding Andreas Baader's escape from Tegel Prison. Here is the text of the communiqué she wrote following their escape:

Our action of May 14 was exemplary because anti-imperialist struggle deals with the liberation of prisoners from the prison, which the system has always signified for all exploited and oppressed groups of the people.

From the imprisonment of total alienation and self-alienation; from political and existential martial law, in which the people are forced to live within the grip of imperialism, consumer culture and the controlling apparatuses of the ruling class.

Direct Action as a means of escaping fate. As every act of terrorism must be, the raid on the Social Institute was "exemplary," a metaphor exploding from the margins onto a much larger screen. Yet Meinhof herself still lived within the confines of discursive language. It was not 'til six years later, when she was incarcerated in a maximum security cell in Stammheim Prison, that she herself became "exemplary."

That she became an Alien, i.e., someone who has changed.

Writing in a secret diary some weeks before her murder-suicide, she was speaking in the same stark cadences she'd once transcribed among the girls back in the Eichenhof:

Feeling your head exploding. Feeling your brain on the point of bursting to bits. Feeling your spine jammed up into your brain and feeling your brain like a dried fruit. Feeling continuously and unconsciously and like an electric wire. Feeling as if they've stolen the associations of your ideas. Feeling your cells move. You open your eyes. The cells move.

At 42, she'd finally come to occupy the same sensate psychic space she'd once longingly observed among incarcerated teenage girls.

AMONG PEOPLE who believe in them, there are those who see the Aliens as hostile and sadistically dispassionate invaders, probing human genitals and anuses with high-tech speculums. It's a little bit like playing s/m, without any of the pleasure.

Just like movies and s/m, Alien Abduction occurs within a kind of five-act structure. The victim is kidnapped from the safety of her home or neighborhood. She struggles uselessly until she's drugged and then unspeakable experiments are performed upon her body. Her identity and will break down. Finally, after withstanding all this torture, she is rewarded with an audience with the Alien-in-Charge.

Invariably, this Alien is male. She notices his superiority

to all the other Aliens: his height, his mental faculties, his extraordinary powers of articulation. She is grateful for the generosity he extends by speaking to her. Considering the demands upon his time and the omniscience of his will and influence, his attention is a precious gift.

The Great Man, ooops, I mean the Alien-in-Charge, then gratifies and torments her with a partial explanation. He tells her things that she'll never fully understand about Alien technology and culture. He says he wants to make her understand the reasons she's been kidnapped. She's been selected as a witness; or perhaps to bear an Alien baby. He drops tantalizing clouded hints about the apocalyptic destiny the Aliens have planned...

In all cases, "knowledge" is transmitted to the victim only through this interview. The sexual encounter, then, is seen to be the price, rather than a conduit of "knowledge." People who fear Aliens are extremely puritanical. Like recovered memory, Alien "experiments" are a shameful and a terrible ordeal. No one ever says, *I was kidnapped by the Aliens and it's the best sex I ever had.*

Other people who believe in Aliens see them as their friends. Invariably, this contact is asexual. The time-frame of their Alien encounters is diffuse and messy, like an experimental film.

Those who look for Alien encounters usually seek them out in groups. One popular belief is that Aliens are attracted by magnetic energies greater than an individual can generate alone. In order to become a group, each person must give up little pieces of themselves. The pieces amplify within a magnet-pool. Cavities in each person's body left by pieces of surrendered ego become receptors for group energy, for

Aliens, the Third Mind.

Thus, the group becomes a self-perpetuating cluster fuck, eating and secreting its own kind.

Generally, these kinds of groups are messy, leaderless and benign. These people look outside themselves for help from Aliens because they're wanting to escape from "the imprisonment of total alienation and self-alienation; from political and existential martial law."

The wartime notebook writings of the philosopher Simone Weil, published posthumously in a book called *Gravity and Grace*, are chronicles of her will to wait for God. In the movie *Gravity & Grace*, a group of earnest lunatics wait for Aliens to rescue them from a New Zealand suburban yard.

Mid-century, late-century. When any of my friend-competitors in New York asked about the film I said, "I'm working on a little movie about God." That usually shut them up.

Millennial countdown: 454 days to go.

THE SECOND screening was scheduled at 3 p.m. on Thursday, and now it was Monday afternoon. The information pack contained a list of all the Market buyers. I found a dingy Chinese restaurant off the Kudaam where I figured they would let me sit all afternoon. Scanning the list, there were about 20 names I vaguely knew. Of them, ten had already seen my work and didn't particularly like it.

But if I couldn't make a movie, writing letters was at least something I knew how to do. I took out the letterhead and press kits and hand-wrote 20 personal letters, varying the pitch according to what I knew about their preferences. Outside it was getting dark and snowing by the time the envelopes were sealed.

I paid the bill and went back over to the Market, thinking to drop the packages in the buyers' mailboxes, but unlike the American Independents, these people had no message pigeonholes. The only way of reaching them was by hand-delivery to their hotels. I took out the map of the central city. The buyers were housed in seven different luxury hotels, spread out within a three-mile radius of the Kudaam. To spend perhaps a hundred dollars on a taxi for this hopeless mission was unthinkable. And so I walked...

Already the sidewalks were calf-deep with snow. But the busy streets were clear, and so I walked the slushy gutters between the Intercontinental and the Regency, the Park Royal, handing packages to the concierges and the doormen. The central city folded all around me like a beaded velvet shawl. Scenes of power, wealth, ambition, glimpsed from the position of a mole – flashing back to working as a messenger my first year in New York City, feeling crazily elated, knowing *this is something I will never do again.*

Gudrun Scheidecker was waiting up when I got back to Kleistpark around 11. She was thrilled to be involved with an American filmmaker who'd been invited to the Festival. She'd told all her friends. And is it not incredible, that in our lifetimes, women now have the same chances to make films as men? She wanted to hear about the first day of the Market – did I go to any parties? – who I talked to, how it went.

Diary entry January 19 at midnight underneath the blankets: *Four more days of this to go.*

CAN MOVIES start with images? Who was it, was it Flaubert who said he wrote the entire novel *Sentimental Education* to evoke the color of a windowsill's peeling paint? He was writing backwards thirty years and I'm imagining that yellow: mustard dulled and deepened by the building's mildew-gray.

Sometime in the late 80s I was back visiting in New Zealand. Everything had changed. Within two years the country had been catapulted fifty years from a sleepy 1940s backwater to an outpost of the New World Order.

As in a Third World country, rapid influxes of global capital had worked this transformation overnight. What was once a social-democratic nation of a xenophobic lower middle class had now been polarized, very rich and very poor. A long cortège of Mercedes Benzes, BMWs, crawled the business capitals. Others walked. When the copper mine shut down in Twizel, the workers' cottages were restyled and sold as weekend skiing condominiums. All government subsidies of butter, milk and mutton – foods which were once considered basic human rights – had been removed. The market, and its attendant New Age ideology of self-actualization, ruled.

My closest friend, the labor leader Eunice Butler, had been removed as head of New Zealand's Accident Compensation Commission. The entire fund had been dissolved. Eunice, a brilliant, charismatic, disciplined politician, now spent her days collecting unemployment, attending astral channeling workshops and questioning herself. What had she done wrong? Was it self-sabotage? Failure, like cancer, can only be a manifestation of a person's secret will.

The landmarks of New Zealand popular culture had mostly disappeared. There were no more rock-hard scones and china mugs at the Railway Station tearooms. They'd all been closed or replaced by franchises for fast food.

Driving north on Highway 2 from Wellington to Masterton, I was listening to a talkback show on Christian radio. A Mother of Three was giving testament to the smug and saved announcer about how God had counseled her to spank her little boy. As in Romania and Guatemala, American-style evangelism had taken off around New Zealand. The woman spoke in that same familiar, querulous New Zealand accent, her voice rising to a question at the end of every sentence, and I wondered about this strange amnesia, how people can remain themselves and still espouse this alien faith.

I got off the road in Silverstream to eat before the Rimutaka Mountains started. The exurban boundaries of Wellington had grown. Once the city stopped at Lower Hutt, and Silverstream had been a country town. But everything was still unfinished, because here, you saw two timescapes shifting, breaking down. There was still a sausage plant and warehouses, a butcher and a hire-purchase store.

At 6 p.m. the town was closed. I drove around and found a takeout burger bar on a side road up the hill. They had a single strand of Xmas lights nailed up along the plateglass window. And everything I'd seen so far congealed into the sadness of those lights –

In the movie *Gravity & Grace*, Ceal Davis, a middle-class New Zealand woman in her 40s, falls off the throughline of her life into despair. She meets a man named Thomas

Armstrong, who believes in flying saucers. "All spring," she tells him, "I've felt on the brink of something, like something's catching in my throat. There's an incredible sadness, but it's a good sadness. I don't want it to go away."

Thomas sees her sadness as a channel. At the close of the European Land Wars in 1862, the Maori prophet Te Ua had a vision on the eve of their defeat that the world would end by flood. At home in her Remuera Tudor, Ceal is contacted by Aliens who tell her that the world will end by flood. Ceal doesn't know if she believes this, but she does.

In 1818, the Massachusetts farmer William Miller predicted through a numerological reading of the Book of Daniel that the world would end within approximately 25 years. He gained the means to spread the word when he converted Joshua Himes, a wealthy businessman, in 1839.

By 1840, thousands of people from the Midwest to New Hampshire were waiting for the midnight cry. Papers, periodicals, pamphlets, tracts and leaflets voicing the coming glory were scattered and broadcast everywhere like autumn leaves. The date was set for April 23 in 1843. That year, camp meetings became so crowded it was impossible to contain the mass hysteria. Cases of insanity were reported. When April 23 came and went, Miller revised his prophecy according to the Jewish calendar. A second date was set: this time, October 22, 1844. Strangely, the first disconfirmation served only to enhance belief.

As Joshua Himes reported, "I have never witnessed a stronger or more active faith." That summer, farmers in New Hampshire refused to plow their fields because the Lord would surely come before another winter. Others, on going to the fields to cut their grass, found themselves unable to proceed and left their crops standing in the field to show their faith. Urban followers sold properties and possessions to leave the world as honorable people, free of debt.

But on the morning of October 23, after waiting up all night, a follower reported to the Boston daily press: "Our fondest hopes and expectations were blasted, and such a weeping came over us as I never experienced before. It seemed the loss of all earthly friends could be no comparison. We wept, and wept, 'til the day dawned."

The second time I saw the movie *Gravity & Grace*, I was living in East Hampton with my husband, driving home from a round of empty errands that had come to fill my days. I was no longer poor, but being poor at least had been a kind of structure, and now I wasn't anyone.

Everything seemed hopeless. It was a rainy afternoon, early November. Bach's *Partita for Cello in B minor*, performed by Ute Uge, came on the radio. I pulled over to the shoulder of Springs Fireplace Road and wept. My skin became so porous that the tremor of the cello crept into my body like an Alien.

This is Ulrike Meinhof speaking to the inhabitants of Earth. You must make your death public. As the rope was tightening around my neck, an Alien made love with me... How does anybody ever figure out their lives? There is a painting in the Frick of St. Francis of Assisi stricken to the ground after being visited by God. He is no longer the gentle saint of birds and animals. The man is totally deranged.

Alien encounters are a phenomenon of marking – pins on the map of an emotional landscape that you'd been moving through but didn't realize had a shape. Despair's a maudlin ecstasy of baroque romanticism. You wait for signs.

THE NEXT day, Tuesday, January 20, I saw no point in going to the Market but it was too cold in Gudrun Scheidecker's apartment to stay home.

I caught the U-Bahn to the Kudaam and went upstairs to check my messages, thinking that if any of the twenty people had responded to my letters it would be nice, but no more probable than life after death.

The pigeonhole was empty. Gordon Laird was deep in conversation with the co-producers of a trailer for a film about some college girls and guys that was doing lots of business. I tried to catch his eye, and failing this, started walking slowly round the trade show floor, carrying the shearling coat and smiling. Up and down the escalators, floors one through four. This went on for about two hours. Finally, I begged the person at the door of Dennis Cooper's *Frisk* to let me sit and watch the movie. I remember being terribly impressed.

A survey conducted by the *Weekly World News* announces that the greatest female fear, surpassing snakes and rodents, is the fear of having to attend a party where you don't know anyone, alone.

That night at the American Independents cocktail party, I circled the room slowly like a Bedouin, holding on to a glass of red wine. Everyone around was tenuously locked in conversation, grasping towards the moment when you run out of things to say. I spent ten minutes talking with the director of the Mill Valley Film Festival, who three months later would reject my film.

The European Film Market was becoming like Room 101 in Orwell's *1984*, a cavalcade of horrors where you confront your deepest fears. And it was so baroque that I was floating just above it, thinking *None of this can hurt me now...*

It was unthinkable to spend another day trying to look busy at the Market. On Wednesday morning I hatched a plan to leave as usual around 8:30 and sneak back into the apartment after Gudrun left for school. But on Wednesday, Gudrun called in sick. Shakily, she told me all about the signs of early menopause. Hot flashes, gripping cramps, the sobbing craziness of waiting for something that never comes –

She closed her bedroom door to sleep. I packed my bags and wrote a note and slipped the keyring under her front door.

Outside, a hailed a taxi to the Hotel Crystal. The name seemed sort of New Age, sort of Nazi. It was a one-star lodging at the bottom of the Market 'recommended' list. A pair of English documentary filmmakers were checking out and thankfully I got their room.

By this time my entire body felt like it was made of glass. I was dying of exposure, couldn't bring myself to check my empty messagebox, smile at Gordon Laird, sit in one more restaurant or cafe alone. I bought a box of crackers and a piece of feta cheese and spent the whole day reading. The radiator purred. A single splotch of sunlight outside the Mansard window moved across the attic walls.

"IT IS impossible," Simone Weil writes in *Gravity and Grace*, "to forgive whoever has done us harm if we believe that harm has lowered us. We have to think that it has not lowered us, but has revealed to us our true level."

She was writing in her notebook in Marseilles in 1942, waiting with her parents not for God but for the US entry visas that her brother Andre Weil, a mathematician already safely in New York, would eventually obtain.

Throughout the war, less than 3,000 French Jews were given entry to America. Weil's educated bourgeois family were among them. 75,000 Jews in France were rounded up during the German occupation and deported. Of them, only three percent survived. In Marseilles, Weil was thinking about the contingencies of chance, all the systems of causality we invent to pretend chance doesn't rule.

"It is intolerable," she wrote, "to suppose that what is most precious in the world should be given over to chance. Therefore, it should be contemplated... The only good which is not subject to chance is that outside the world –" Although, as Weil well knew, the rich have always been more "lucky" than the poor.

Weil found the safety of New York unbearable. She dreamt of being parachuted back to France among the Nazis. All her life since she was 10 she'd empathized with the poor and dispossessed. It was a panic of altruism. She felt the suffering of others in her body, and found a language and a system for it. Value, she decided, exists only in the joining of two previously separate things. Value ceases when that union is dissolved. Craving unity, she launched herself into an altruistic panic, a state in which there aren't any boundaries between who you are and what you see.

"A man whose family had died under torture," she wrote later on in London, "who had himself been tortured for a long time in a concentration camp, or a 16th century Indian, the sole survivor after the total extermination of his people, such men, if they had previously believed in the mercy of God would either believe in it no longer, or else they would conceive of it quite differently. I have not been through such things. *I know, however, that they exist, so what is the difference?*"

Because she herself was brilliant, she sought to discredit the value of intelligence. "The intelligent man who is proud of his intelligence is like a condemned man who is proud of his large cell…" *(London Notebooks)*

The overarching project of Weil's writing, which fills some 15 volumes published half a century later by Editions Gallimard, was to find the points of intersection between Mahayana Buddhism and the early Greeks. Weil saw Greek culture as the roots of Western thought. According to the Greek scholar Pierre Vidal-Naquet, her entire comprehension of Greek culture was crazy and ecstatic, flawed.

Weil was more a mystic than a theologian. That is, all the things she wrote were field notes for a project she enacted on herself. She was a performative philosopher. Her body was material. "The body is a lever for salvation," she thought in *Gravity and Grace*. "But in what way? *What is the right way to use it?*"

There is something just so ludicrous about a female mystic, especially one who is contemporary. In 1942 she left New York for London, where she lived and worked for 15 months before dying of tubercular starvation at the age of 34. "She talks of suffering atrocious pain for others, 'those who are indifferent or unknown to me,' …and it is almost as if a comic character from Dickens were speaking," wrote Graham Greene. Alain, her teacher at Lycèe Henri IV, affectionately called Simone an Alien. Her nickname was "the Martian."

Until recently, nearly all the secondary texts on Simone Weil treat her philosophical writings as a kind of biographic key. Impossible to conceive a female life that might extend outside itself. Impossible to accept the self-destruction of a woman as strategic. Weil's advocacy of decreation is read as evidence of her dysfunction, her hatred-of-her-body, etc.

There is a medieval mystical tradition which defines the self as "a foul stinking lump" that must be broken down. Weil takes this one step further, as a woman living in the mid-20th century: it isn't just the second-person self she's seeking to destroy. She's starting with the one she knows the best, her own.

"If the 'I' is the only thing we truly own, we must destroy it," she writes in *Gravity and Grace*. "Use the 'I' to break down 'I'."

She wants to lose herself in order to be larger than herself. A rhapsody of longing overtakes her. She wants to really see. Therefore, she's a masochist.

"There is a reality," she wrote in London, "beyond the world, that is to say, outside space and time, outside any sphere that is accessible to human faculties. Corresponding to this reality in the center of the human heart, is the longing for *an absolute good...*"

The scholar Nancy Houston faults Weil for her denial of the body. She pities her because she never fucked, and therefore must've suffered from a lack of self-esteem. It's as if, because there were so few women speaking to her time, Weil must be judged only as some kind of role model, "a credit to her race."

According to Weil's English editor/biographer, Richard

Rees, she identifies the chief value of the human soul as a state of utter impersonality. And yet, as her friend-enemy Simone de Beauvoir would later argue in *The Second Sex*, the female self, because it is primarily defined by gender, can never be perceived impersonally.

In his 1991 biography of Weil, the scholar Thomas Nevin writes: "Her intellectual rigor, her relentless, never concessive way of arguing a position, her quest for the pure, worked as mechanisms for distancing herself as others might see her, as a woman." (*Simone Weil: Portrait of a Self-Exiled Jew*)

In an extraordinarily patronizing introduction to Mary McCarthy's translation of Weil's monograph, *The Iliad – A Poem of Force*, Weil's brother Andre notes that if only she had combed her hair, worn stockings and high heels, the world might have taken her more seriously.

Her work was "odious," her friend-enemy Georges Bataille wrote six years after her death, "immoral, trite, irrelevant and paradoxical."

The bibliographic sourcebook to Weil's work, published by UC Santa Cruz in 1992, describes her as an "anorexic philosopher" who died of self-starvation at the age of 34. Weil as the brilliant crazy girl, the awkward scarecrow in flat shoes, the self-loathing and self-starving androgyne.

THERE IS a tendency among romantic people to see their lives as grids and mazes, unfolding through an erratic but connected set of lines. These randomly occurring series of causalities may be retrospectively observed to *form a pattern...*

And so, as the philosophers Deleuze and Guattari surmise from reading William Burroughs, the idea of chance becomes a kind of fairy tale. Chance as a means of trumping chaos, discovering a more deeply comprehensive *secret* unity in the world.

In the Brownie Handbook there was a game we used to play called "Penny Walk." You go outside, and at every corner, flip a coin. For heads turn left, for tails turn right. If coincidence is charmed, can chance be fatal? When you don't know what to do, you look for signs.

Signs are miracles, appearing when we least expect them, at moments when the conscious mind has given up, turned off. Signs appear in many forms: found objects and lost property, a stranger's words.

In 1453 the London Midwives Guild published a list of signs that told the plague was near. *When ravens gather at the edge of fields, and babies cry before the dusk...* You are walking along Third Avenue near East 53rd Street in Manhattan after applying for some job. You reach into your pocket, realize you don't have enough money for the subway. You pass a dumpster filled with trash and see a book. You open it: page 3-5-3, the coordinates on which you're standing, and that page tells you everything you need to know about your life. Time and circumstance has led you to this moment of exhaustion. The Tao of Dereliction: wanting to attain a state in which you may be porous: mobile, lost and penniless and constantly alert.

Andre Breton equates his search for beauty with his pursuit of crazy Nadja. He is at his desk, she is in a mental hospital in the Vaucluse. He talks about experiencing a "shock," the "royalty of silence."

Throughout the 20th century, chance has repeatedly recurred as the basis of artistic practice among groups of highly educated men. Man Ray photographs Robert Desnoes during the "Nap Period" at the Surrealist Headquarters, a suite of rooms in a hotel owned by one of the Surrealist's dads. In the picture, Desnoes looks like a wild and crazy guy, his eyeballs rolling, reaching towards the ceiling through his head. (Although he'd also be "unlucky" later, deported by the Germans in 1942…)

In Zurich, 1917, Hugo Ball and Tristan Tzara made nonsense poems of glossolalia. They were trying, Ball's Dada manifesto said, "to get rid of all the filth that clings to this accursed language." In New York during the early 1960s, John Cage and Fluxus members made random compositions out of sound and gestures. In London at the Empress Hotel, Brion Gysin, William Burroughs and Ian Sommerville invented "cut-up" text and movies, their intuition forced like tulip bulbs to reveal the hidden messages in what we hear and see.

These men were crocodiles in clubchairs, conductors of controlled experiments in chaos. In the interest of a greater science they were prepared to gouge out pieces of their own non-porous skin. Girls, on the other hand, are less reptilian…

Katia Perry liked to hitch-hike up and down the North Island of New Zealand between Wellington and Auckland. Hitch-hiking was a game of chance. Because at that time Katia was reading English at the university and lacked the critical intelligence to perceive any difference between herself and what she read, she imagined hitch-hiking as a picaresque adventure.

Tom Jones became the master-text. Each ride that Katia

hitched was the beginning of a new digressive chapter, beginning with the words "In Which..." Highway 1 from Wellington to Auckland was like a magic-box of postmodernity. It was a two-lane road spanning 350 miles and in the course of it the landscape changed from rain forest to desert and everything in between.

In Otaki where the rolling hills were English-green, she liked to make believe the pick-up she was riding was a stagecoach. North of Palmerston when the heather bushes gathered into forest, Katia wandered through the northern provinces of 17th century Japan. She was the poet Basho on a pilgrimage. In Taihape the sheep-filled hills would narrow into skyward-pointing crooked rocks like Flemish cliffs in a medieval painting. On this journey anything could happen, and Katia's ambition was to use her lifetime to learn everything there was to know.

Traveling through continents and centuries, Katia liked to look for signs and messages. The fact that she was hitchhiking meant these messages would arrive from people who she didn't know. And didn't her favorite poet, James K. Baxter, warn to keep your front door open to a stranger because the stranger might be Christ?

One Sunday Katia caught a ride from Wellington to Silverstream. The next ride took her fifty miles to a turn-off north of Dannevirke. The road was empty and she walked for several miles. It was a transitional place where farmland started sharpening to mountains. The hills were ragged, etched with muddy ridges trod by sheep. The highway cut between the hilltops through a valley. It was springtime cold and damp and *water trickled down the rocks and leapt across the road.*

Katia was hoping to arrive in Taupo, a lake resort with twenty cheap motels, by dark but at 3:30 this was seeming doubtful. So when three drunks in a battered Ford pulled up and offered her a ride she thought she ought to go. A farm manager and his wife had brought her here from Silverstream; this ride was a jumpcut into another social realm. What was that line that Katia remembered? *Be prepared to meet the stranger for the stranger might be Christ.* Katia had a vivid sense of Jesus, his arms stretched out into the blood-red clouds behind the Wairarapa hills.

She threw her knapsack in the car and debated whether beer's a sacrament when the driver put his arm around her. *What is a sacrament? A sacrament is an outward and visible sign of an inward and spiritual grace...* It was romantic: four strangers lumbering down the highway in this 1960s car. They offered her a drink and then a pill and she accepted, listening to their country accents. Their voices jumbled up between the bad reception of the radio, drifting in and out. Blobby specks of sheep were scattered all around the hills. There was a famous poem about the sheep by Allen Curnow – *the sheep spread like a pestilence along the hillside* – Katia smiled. The sun was making its last call as they traveled down the bumpy road.

The pill was making everything extended. Katia noticed that they must've left the highway because they were heading down an unsealed road. No one was talking. A low white house came into view: a shearer's quarters? There was a satellite antenna, several cars and music blasting through the open doors and windows. It was a party. The driver said We're here, and Katia followed as the guys got out and went inside.

What she noticed was the furniture. How even though it was mismatched and shabby there were traces of a grandmother kind of feeling. Inside there was a couple and two other guys, some talking. The ones who picked her up were guests. A fat and bearded guy in jeans seemed to be the one in charge. Eventually the couple wandered off alone.

Katia didn't know if she was tripping but she started picturing the bearded guy as if he was Roland, the Bandit King in de Sade's *Justine*. Blinking back and forth between these times and places, she was completely unaware of her own presence in the picture. Therefore, she saw no danger or that she was a tripping teenage girl with five drunk men. Later on the afternoon dissolved into a haze of furniture and floor and bruises. But Katia crawled out, survived –

MY FRIEND Dan Asher arrived back in New York City in early 1978. He'd been living for some time in Paris, taking photographs of bums and rock stars and Bejart ballerinas, sometimes staying in some friends' apartments, sometimes sleeping by the Seine. I don't remember where we met – maybe a coffeeshop, maybe the Gem Spa – the word "homeless" hadn't been invented yet, but he didn't have a place to live and I thought he was a genius, i.e., we hated many of the same people, so I invited him to stay with me. Dan Asher on the art world: "I'd rather be with the bums, the clochards, they're more interesting than the jerk-offs who run the culture industry!"

Dan wore a baggy overcoat and was always getting into fights with people. It was only later that he defined his condition as 'autistic,' a condition that he's since talked and written about incisively. I just accepted he was crazy, I was crazy too and so we got along. I'd fallen in with this group of people who'd gone to school at Swarthmore, Harvard and Grinnell. Dan and I were part of their transitional urban landscape, a demimonde that they'd eventually outgrow. Already in their mid-20s they were having tortured conversations about their futures. They were ridiculous, like the assholes in that book by Jean-Paul Sartre *The Age of Reason*. It was obvious to us there was no future. Punk suited us very well.

Dan was taking photos for some people at a magazine he hated. I was acting in a play. Often the director would look at me and say, *I want you to be more vulnerable*, which was a total joke. I had no money and no prospects for ever getting money. The only way I knew of paying rent was giving blowjobs in the backs of topless bars; whereas the director was receiving an allowance from his parents and had just graduated from Grinnell. Dan didn't mind it that I played the Poly Styrene record, *Oh Bondage Up Yours* about thirty times a day.

My roommate Tom, who was studying philosophy at the New School, slept in the bedroom, I slept in the storeroom, Dan slept on the couch. We got up around 11 after Tom had gone to school and spent hours laughing up our sleeves at everyone we knew. The apartment was completely aboriginal. It was our cave. Sometimes our conversations got so intense that I'd get up and buy a set of poster paints to write aphorisms of our thoughts inside the cupboards, on the walls.

Mostly we talked about how everything was so transparent. All that motivated anybody on the bullshit New

York punk scene was their careers or fucking. The girls were worst, because mostly all they had was fucking. Stuffed into black leather fishnet outfits, leaning back against club walls they were pro bono whores, wanting all the coolest boys to love them. When I wasn't topless dancing I wore an army surplus uniform. It was beyond me why anyone would want to show their tits for free. Dan, in his baggy overcoat, was immune to anything to do with sex, found it basically disgusting. It cracked us up, how all these people were pretending to be in a state of permanent rebellion but all they really cared about was validation. Dan hated all the straight-boy rock stars. What moved us most were symbolic acts of violence and destruction. We were a two-person Junior Anti-Sex League.

Dan was broke but he wanted to go back to France. Some guy he'd met had offered to cut him in on a business proposition, but he needed about 500 bucks to front it. I worked some extra dancing shifts but then the product disappeared. When his mother finally bought his ticket, Dan felt guilty leaving without paying back the money so he left behind a cardboard box of stuff that he'd been carting round the world.

"Here Chris you can keep this box," he rasped, the morning that the plane was leaving and then I didn't see him for another twenty years.

Long ago and far away in a country something like Japan there lived a peasant man who kept a swallow as a pet. His wife was a mean and jealous woman. She thought her husband was a fool to feed the bird on scraps of his own scanty meals. One day when she was ironing, the swallow flew in through the window and knocked over a bottle of starch. The wife grabbed her broom and hit the bird and told it never to come back again.

When the man heard this he put on his boots and coat and set off into the woods to find the swallow. And after he had trudged long and weary through the forest, he stopped for a moment to catch his breath. And a messenger swallow alighted on his shoulder from a tree and beckoned him to into a clearing. The man hesitated for a moment, but then he went. And when he got into the clearing he saw a house – a straw house, flecked with silver and with gold. It was the finest house the man had ever seen.

A woman stepped out of the straw house. She was tall, with long black hair and softly solemn eyes. She told her cooks to prepare a banquet, she told her ladies-in-waiting to dance before the man. And after all the eating and the dancing, the woman stepped forward and revealed herself to the man. She said, The swallow is but one of my many forms.

You were very kind to me. Your kindness shall be repaid.

I missed him. Weeks passed before I got around to opening the box. And when I did, there was a set of photographs he took of Patti Smith, Keith Richards, Tom Verlaine. Some beads and feathers. And then a pile of books: the writings of the Dadaist Hugo Ball, some books in French by Antonin Artaud. Plon's first edition of Simone Weil's *Gravity and Grace*, in French, *La Pesanteur et la grace*. The writings of Ulrike Meinhof, including Meinhof's screenplay translated into French as *Le Foyer*. I bought a dictionary, started reading.

Though it hadn't yet occurred to me to be an artist, Dan's box contained everything I'd work on. And this took 15 years.

CHANCE AND magic, chance and claustrophobia.

On Thursday afternoon I got out of bed and went back to the Market for the $300 screening. Twelve people came. The most notable was the director of the Boston Jewish Women's Film Festival, who later took the time to write a personal rejection. As the lights went down, I did the math. Factoring in the airfare and hotel and Market fees, each of them was watching *Gravity & Grace* at a personal cost to me of about $275. Nine left before the reel change. I realized that *Gravity & Grace* would actually've played much better nearly anywhere but here. Two people left during the second reel, and when the lights came up, only one remained. His name was Thomas Niederkorn.

He introduced himself as a German living in New York. He'd studied film at NYU. Thomas Niederkorn was 25, well groomed and classy in a classless kind of way. He said he was an independent film producer, having meetings at the Market to raise money for a feature. It seemed incredible that he'd sat through the entire film. My heart leapt when he said the word *producer*.

"I'd like to ask you something," Thomas said.

"Yes? –" I smiled expectantly.

"If you're maybe still in contact with a New Zealand friend of mine. Her name is Delphine Bower."

I knew lots about Delphine Bower. Her name was listed on the end credits of *Gravity & Grace* as Associate Producer. Given the nature and circumstances of Delphine's participation, crediting her was my final act of martyrdom to the movie. Or so I thought –

"Ahh, she was extraordinary," Thomas said. "I think she is a genius. She was so beautiful and giving. Delphine helped me shoot the pilot for my thriller. For six months she was my girlfriend. And when she left, we parted friends." Thomas wondered if I'd seen her.

Silently I computed. It was now the end of January, '96. Delphine Bower had disappeared for good two days after we'd finished shooting in New York; November '93. (She'd actually walked off the set during the first or second day of shooting, but she came back the final week to consciousness-raise among the cast and crew about how callously they'd been exploited, and, oh yes, run up another $300 international long distance on our phone –) Now, if Thomas shot his pilot in the Fall of '95, that meant Delphine must've actually hung around New York for two more years. For an orphan from a Taranaki trailer park without a green card or a job, this amounted to a triumph.

Perversely and dispassionately I'd kept tabs on Delphine's movements until the end of '94. Fascinating to chart the movement of a given subject, "Delphine B.," through concentric circles of the New York art world. Her movements traced a kind of sociogram. News of the subject's movements filtered back from Harlem and Tribeca long after she'd burned through our immediate acquaintances. The flight patterns of "Delphine B." were like a game of free association among interlocking sets of friends and personalities and acquaintances. Because she left behind a trail of mystery, stolen objects, lies and unpaid bills, most everyone remembered her. The last I'd heard of "Delphine B.," she'd been sighted making xeroxes in the offices of *Artforum*.

If Delphine had worked with Thomas in the Fall, that meant she'd been there nine more months than were accounted for. I felt a queasy bitterness at Thomas' mention of her name. Part of me was tempted to tell him everything.

THE FIRST time I met Delphine Bower was in New Zealand, January 1993. I fell in love and she was lovable. It'd been my fantasy all that Fall, living with my husband, Sylvère Lotringer, in Easton, Pennyslvania to save money for the film, that in New Zealand I would finally have a girlfriend. I pictured her a baby-butch with rosy cheeks, maybe a motorbike, a younger version of my friend Darlene. She'd take me round to all the bars and make it possible to make a movie. For the past two years I'd had a chills-and-goosebumps crush on a student of my husband's who thought it was the ultimate frisson, seducing her professor's wife. But then she laughed at me, it came to nothing.

Last summer, Delphine had starred in a long experimental movie by Jason Pauling. Jason fell in love with her. She was a vibrant dewey 20. Since then, she'd dropped out of university and didn't have a job or place to live and when Jason tried to have an earnest talk with her about her future, Delphine said, "But all I really want is to make movies." Jason was hoping I'd find a job for her. She had a flair with clothes… perhaps she could assist with wardrobe?

When we talked, Delphine immediately got me on her side by making fun of Jason's looks, paternalism and his movie. I'd only been in Auckland for two weeks but already felt like I was running for elected office, scrounging favors, being nice, so Delphine's meanness was a delicious rush. For the first time since arriving in New Zealand, Delphine made me feel I was connecting.

We met downtown. She was already waiting at the trendy downtown bistro, bored and playing with *faux*-pearls. Her hair was cut like Louise Brooks. She wore a double-breasted pinstripe jacket. Delphine wanted me to like her and I did. She was adorable but with an edge; performing with the softest, most deliberate sense of irony. Delphine Bower was no eager film-crew girl jock. She enacted the humiliating role of "job-seeker" with a self-reflexive nod. Moving back and forth between a savage parody of Jason and a touchingly ingenuous enthusiasm for my script, Delphine emitted a vapor of compassionate disdain for a world that couldn't help but disappoint her. She was a genius tossed upon a world that had no place for working class girl geniuses. And then, she was emotionally frail and beautiful –

By the second drink it became unthinkable to waste Delphine on anything as insignificant as wardrobe. We talked through a list of film crew jobs. They all fell short. Therefore, the only thing to do was make her co-producer. Quickly, it was arranged that Delphine would move into my Grey Lynn townhouse in exchange for working on the movie. She'd use my car and I'd pay all of her expenses.

For months Delphine was unfailingly efficient and good company. I started to revise this idea I'd had, of "girlfriend." Delphine was a pretty girl and not a baby-butch. She treated me like mom, so clearly sex between us was unthinkable. But she was radiant and charming. While I'd never *been* a pretty girl, why not become like all the men I was competing with and *have* one?

Delphine told me stories while we worked the phones. Orphaned at birth, she'd been adopted by a Taranaki couple. Her adopted father died when she was 12, and Vi, her mom, took up with a hard-drinking flannel-shirted dyke named Di. Vi and Di raised young Delphine in a trailer park and taught her how to bet on dogs. She did a wicked imitation of the two of them, prompted by her mom's gift-packages and letters.

The later stories of Delphine Bower concerned the fates of boys who'd fallen tragically in love with her. There was the Young Medical Student who'd killed himself when 16 year old Delphine rejected him. (All Delphine's antagonists were named by rank, not name, like characters in a medieval allegory.) When Delphine heard the news she cried until she was hospitalized and sedated. On the third night Delphine pried open an unlocked window at the sanatorium. She climbed the trellis to the ground and caught a bus to Auckland. Delphine was Nadja, she was Rapunzel. I was so entranced by this that I forgot there was no "medical school" within 300 miles of Taranaki…

Meanwhile Delphine made fantastic progress setting up the movie. In Auckland, she'd been virtually re-adopted by her prep-school boyfriend Dodge's wealthy Remuera family. And while Delphine had begun to sense the *limits* of weedy Dodge and his nouveau-riche provincial family, for our purposes they were very well connected. She conned the Sunday-painting wife of an investment banker into loaning us their Remuera home to use as primary location. When Delphine was on, no one could say no to her. She was the insouciantly stylish anarchist that her victims longed to be. And this was coupled, sometimes, with a sense of gratitude, respect, accountability. As the production grew from just the two of us to a horde of eager young professionals for whom our movie was no different from any movie-of-the-week or Lexus spot, Delphine was my only confidante and ally.

The first sign things were starting to go wrong came two days after hiring a real production manager. Delphine got drunk, parked on a hill and forgot to use the handbrake on my car. The vintage Morris Minor slammed into the back of some guy's Toyota Celica. It was so transparently a test. Did I still love her? Of course I only loved her more. I paid the bill, about $1200.

People who knew Delphine started warning me she was dangerous and incompetent. And she began to prove them right. One night when Delphine was driving, Jason Pauling's prize possession, a $2,000 Nagra, vanished mysteriously from the car. But seeing her was still my only pleasure. So when the US funds came through to shoot the last part of the movie in New York, I bought Delphine a ticket on Air France. While it was cheaper, United seemed too tacky.

The last night we spent together in New Zealand we watched *Three Women*, Delphine's favorite film, by Robert Altman. It seemed a little creepy. As if the only possible relationship that women can invent together is familial, Mother-Daughter-Sister. Still, that night I loaned Delphine my car. Until she joined me in New York some five months later she'd be alone with no one to look after her. I couldn't bear to see her walk or ride the bus. At first Sylvère objected, but he had a child and I had no one to take care of. Delphine and the Morris Minor were the only two New Zealand things I truly loved, so it seemed fitting they should be together. The night before she left for New York City she got drunk. As Delphine told it, she pulled over on downtown Queen

Street and passed out at 5 a.m. When the cops arrived she left the key in the ignition. The car was never seen again.

While in New Zealand I'd been Delphine's cherished older friend, it was apparent in New York that I'd become another Dodge: an obstacle to her mobility and freedom. She borrowed money, disappeared, returned, and lied. She ran up huge long distance phone bills. Delphine's success in parlaying bar sex into money and protection was astonishing. I'd thought her pouty lips and baby fat, her ultra-femme flirtation, wouldn't cut it in New York but I was wrong. Within two weeks of arriving in New York, she had a handful of employed and lovestruck guys competing for her.

Meanwhile I was left to deal with how to shoot a 40 minute section of the film for $20,000; how to house the New Zealand cast and crew who'd be arriving in October; how to buy the film to shoot the 1:9 ratio Colleen, the New Zealand Director of Photography, who until now had focus-pulled on TV dramas and commercials, demanded.

Delphine seduced everyone I introduced her to. Doug Harvey, a close friend of ten years, begged her to ditch the film and fly back to LA with him. Sensing there were better opportunities yet to come, she told me about Doug's offer. I roared as Delphine imitated my good friend's reticence and WASP good manners. Doubts gathered but broke down each time Delphine showed up sobbing in the morning.

By this time it was completely clear that Delphine wasn't going to do anything to help the movie. The only question was how to contain the damages. Just as I was gathering the courage to get rid of her, the New Zealand cast and crew arrived from Auckland. In my absence Delphine had moved in with Colleen Sweeney, the Director of Photography.

Colleen had become Delphine's new protectress, and she was horrified that I would turn an orphan out onto the streets of New York City. Together, Delphine-Colleen convinced the cast and crew whose salaries Sylvère and I were paying that we were heartless money-grubbing Jews and monsters.

On the sixth day of production, Colleen tried to mobilize a walk-out strike because Sylvère and I refused to pay for caterers. By the twelfth day Colleen and Harriet, the $600 p/wk AD fresh out of experimental film school, banned me from riding in my own car which had become the "production vehicle." Each night Sylvère and I cruised the outer reaches of the Bronx in search of cheap hotels so that Delphine-Colleen could be alone and run up long distance bills in our apartment. Laughs and whispers stopped abruptly whenever I walked onto the set. My commitment to hiring a mostly-female cast and crew had turned the movie into a nightmare reprise of junior high school. On Saturday, I played hostess to Colleen, took her around New York. Because both of us were girls, she had a talk with me about my problems. "Really," Colleen said, "you ought to do some work around the issues that you have surrounding money."

Three days after they all went home I was resting in East Hampton. Driving aimlessly around the back roads, I blacked out behind the wheel. The front end of the car was smashed; I have no idea what happened.

Discounting the New Zealand car repair, Delphine Bower's total cost had been about $6,000. According to our Visa bill (she had my card) Delphine stayed on in the East Village, buying gourmet food and makeup. But when I stopped the card her trail cooled off. She'd stayed with Carol Irving, the New York production manager, several days, stealing clothes and heirloom jewelry. Following that, she sublet Carol's friend Jayce's place on Avenue B and skipped out owing two month's rent and phone bills. From there, who knows? She had a passionate affair with a student of my friend Ann Rower and was living in his dorm room for a while. Months later I heard from a distant friend that Delphine Bower had been living with a Russian Poet who'd tragically been shot to death in Harlem. So I just assumed that Delphine had gone back to New Zealand, except that Carol Irving heard that she'd been sighted working on a cable show about the art world, and then we heard from someone else that Delphine was now an intern at *Artforum*. Was this Delphine Bower's final triumph?

Delphine's story was apocryphal. For months I'd thought of making her the subject of a movie. I'd hire a private investigator to track her down. This time we'd shoot in Hi-8 video. By interviewing all of Delphine's victims, a portrait of the city would emerge. She was the thread connecting many worlds and characters. Her story was like Balzac; it was like Fellini's *Roma*. I wrote a bunch of grant proposals. None were funded.

And so I looked at Thomas Niederkorn, nodded and smiled blankly. The Delphine Bower Story was my precious hoard. Obviously he was disappointed.

I never went back to the Market. The next day while the film was screening to an audience of maybe thirty, maybe three, I walked around the Berlin Kunstmuseum. There was a show of black and white photos from the Holocaust; sort of a recycled *Shoah*. It didn't interest me. In the museum store, there was a catalogue for a show by an artist named Paul Thek that'd been and gone called *The Wonderful World That Almost*

Was. The man behind the counter said in English it was the most amazing show he'd ever seen and I should buy it.

On the twentieth of January Lenz went through the mountains. It was cold and damp; the water trickled down the rocks and leapt across the road. The clouds, like wild, neighing horses, sprang forward, and the sun shone through them and penetrated the snowfields with its glittering sword, so that a bright, blinding light cut its way down from the summits into the valleys.

I went back to the Crystalnacht Hotel and started reading.

The chronology at the back quoted a postcard Thek had written sometime in the late 70s, to the photographer Peter Hujar in New York: "Life is getting longer. I smoke dope, I fall in love with living." Peter Hujar was a person who I almost knew; he'd been the lover, friend and mentor of someone I knew, the artist David Wojnarowicz. Back in New York City and alone in 1986, Paul Thek wrote another postcard, this time to Franz Deckwitz: "I spend most of my time these days in what could be called a 'highly toxic' condition. Smoking a lot of grass..." Peter Hujar died of AIDS in 1987; David tested positive in 1989 and died in summer, 1992. Thek tested positive in 1986 and died of AIDS in 1988.

And here begins the difficult task of trying to understand another person.

2.

IN 1966 Paul Thek was 33 years old. The age Christ lived to be. It's an age that many men experience significantly, as a landmark. That year Thek had a show of his *Technological Reliquaries*, wax replicas of animal and human meat encased in glass, at Pace Gallery in New York. In an artworld atmosphere of anti-censorship, Thek's show was taken as polemic, a shock-assault on people's senses. Confronted with cross-sections of striated flesh, "people literally get sick," the reviewer for *Art News* said. Although this wasn't Thek's intention. He was floating someplace else, outside the orbit of the literal humanism of his time. He was a pantheist in search of radical detachment.

"Everything," he said that year, "is beautiful and ugly simultaneously. We accept our thing-ness intellectually, but the emotional acceptance of it can be a joy."

Three years ago, he'd visited the Capuchin catacombs near Palermo and was amazed to see 8,000 corpses – "not skeletons, *corpses*" – decorating the walls. He'd picked up what he thought to be a piece of paper. It was a human thigh. Touching it made him feel strangely relieved and free. "It delighted me that bodies could be used to decorate a room, like flowers."

One of the pieces in this show called *Birthday Cake* presents a four-tiered pyramid of human flesh adorned with soft-pink birthday candles. Art writers sought to distance the emotional implications of Thek's work by comparing it to French surrealism, an art movement he despised. Dreams bored him. Thek didn't see himself creating object-poems with symbols drawn from the unconscious. He wanted to be hyper-conscious. Years later, when he'd left the New York artworld and was staging spectacles, processions that involved entire European villages and towns, he talked about creating something called a "social Surrealism." "Everything," Thek said, "must be looked at closely." He wanted to remain alert.

In an interview conducted for *Art News* in 1966, G.R. Swenson wanted to engage Paul Thek in a psychological reading of his work. Really, Swenson wondered, aren't you saying that like God, the "individual in art" is dead? "Individualism doesn't interest me," Thek answered.

"But yet," Swenson countered, "I've seen your work produce strong subjective states –" "Which I want people to rise above," Thek said. "I know it's weird to see a piece of flesh hanging on the wall. I choose this subject matter because it violates my sensibilities, but that's not the same thing as shock. I work with it to detach myself from it, like a heartbeat."

Thek, who was ambivalently homosexual, was arguing for a state of decreation, a plateau at which a person might, with all their will and consciousness, become a thing. "The chief element of value in the soul is its *impersonality*," wrote Simone Weil. Among people who reject the mystical state, the only yardstick left for measuring the will-to-decreate is sadomasochism. Thek, a male, acting upon wax, Swenson thought, must be sadistic... just as Weil's detractors saw her, a female, acting on herself, as masochistic. Though neither of them really saw the world through these polarities. They were someplace else, arguing for an alien-state, using subjectivity as a means of breaking out of time and space –

Years later in an *Artforum* interview with Richard Flood, when his adversarial position to the artworld had permanently hardened, Thek reinterpreted his meat-works as a big Fuck You to minimalism, the institutionalized art movement of that time:

"The name of the game seemed to be 'how cool can you be' and 'how refined.' Nobody ever mentioned anything that seemed real. The world was falling apart, anyone could see it. I was a wreck, the block was a wreck, the city was a wreck; and I'd go to a gallery and there'd be a lot of people looking at stuff that didn't say anything about anything to anyone..."

This was in 1981. Twelve years later Thek's meat-pieces were revisited in the work of Damien Hirst. Discussing *Mother and Child Divided* (1993) in which two cows are sliced in half and sandwiched between glass in a formaldehyde solution, Hirst told interviewer Stuart Morgan that he wanted to create emotions scientifically.

"What's sad," Hirst said, "is that if you look at my cows cut-up in formaldehyde, they have more personality than any cows walking about in fields... It's the banal animal that gives it the emotion." Hirst's cows are flesh without any complex sentimental yearning towards transcendence. When Morgan asked him about dead people, where they are, Hirst simply says: "They are not."

"Nobody noticed," Thek said in 1981, "that I was working with the hottest subject known to man, the human body, and doing it in a totally controlled way, which I thought was the required distancing..." The problem that both men encountered was that their meat pieces became an autograph. Hirst realized this in 1996. In 1966, when people around Soho started recognizing Paul Thek as "the meat man," he stopped. And so instead of casting hunks of flesh in wax encased in plexiglass, Thek cast himself as human corpse.

The Tomb, shown at Stable Gallery in New York in 1967,

was Thek's first environmental installation. He is a thin man wearing jeans, a necklace and a double breasted blazer lying on a grungey bier. His head is resting on two pillows, face up. Beside him are three cups (the Three of Cups?). There are a few sheets of paper on the ground, a few handwritten pages of a letter hastily taped behind his head up on the wall.

That year a curator at the Whitney renamed the sculpture *Death of a Hippie*. And that became the piece's definition. It was a well-timed marketing coup. At that moment, *Death of a Hippie* was one of the few pieces of high art that had a topicality beyond the claustrophobia referencing of art criticism. While Watts burned, the art world was considering the antecedence of minimalism over pop. Years later, *Death of a Hippie* would be read as a response to Altamont and Manson's Family. Like Robert Stone's classic novel of the period *Dog Soldiers*, *Death of a Hippie* placed the enchanted hippie dream within the realm of true Americana: criminal burnout, guns, hard drugs and sleaze.

In his essay *Death and Transfiguration*, Mike Kelley argues brilliantly for Thek's place in a forgotten canon, art that took place within the counterculture and has since been disappeared. Art history, Kelley writes, has historicized the 1960s as a period that was "in touch with the national identity... the last glory of Modernism before the Fall."

The Reagan-Bush ideology of the artworld, Kelley writes, has exiled all the artworks that reflect the 60s as "a period of dirt, mysticism, drugs and anarchy." Kelley sees *Death of a Hippie* as Thek's master-work, which "tackles head-on the very material Warhol shuns in his gallery work... the 'tripping corpse' speaks an American language, a low and dirty language... It must because it is speaking to those who are frightened of the low and dirty... [and have] positioned YOU as low and dirty... It is [America's] fear of death." And because of this, Thek's work has been exiled from the continuum of art history. Because his work is difficult to place within art history's sanctioned framework, he is an anomaly, an admirable freak.

Thek, perversely, later claimed not to have been thinking any of these thoughts at all. Ambivalently Catholic, he was wondering about transfiguration. "The Tomb never had anything to do with hippies," he wrote in a postcard to Robert Pincus Witten. "The press started all that."

But who will know, because like most of Paul Thek's installation artifacts and objects, The Tomb no longer exists. It was damaged by a shipper in 1981, and then destroyed when Thek refused to pay the bill.

The artist Christiana Glidden staged a kind of recreation of The Tomb in her installation Hades (1998). The artist, this time a young woman, lying in state in an empire-waisted dress and ruby slippers. Her lightly rouged and penciled wax-acrylic face appears so real that you are waiting for the corpse's breath but nothing happens. Lying there as beautiful as pre-Raphaelite Ophelia, drowning in the painting by Millais, she is resting on a slab that feels like a launching pad into the underworld. The piece is beautiful and frightening. You wish her well.

In 1968 Thek went to Europe on a Fulbright and then he had a show in Amsterdam. Though he didn't plan to leave forever, he wouldn't live and work in the US again for nine more years. In Munich he saw the incredible felt and tallow-wax sledge sculptures made by Joseph Beuys. Working in wax and quoting St. John's Gospel, Beuys in many ways was Paul Thek's psychic twin. He loved and hated him. Later on he talked about how Beuys' work seemed "really ponderous... totally devoid of wit or humor or grace... It seemed to me that all it needed was glamour and worth and charm and a woman's touch."

By the late 1970s, both men were doing what they called "performances." I witnessed one of Beuys', and it was a very paramilitary affair. The Great Man arrived flanked by a cadre of disciples, young men in orange jumpsuits who served as secretary-acolytes. This particular performance was staged as a "town meeting." Its goal, as far as I can tell, was to create an international network of Beuys-followers, or perhaps to prove the impossibility of achieving anything through talk at all. At that time, Beuys was positing a dichotomy between Marxism and spirituality. The "meeting" quickly turned into a shouting match between Soho gallerists, Beuys' acolytes, and a bunch of male East Village leftists who claimed to represent "the workers." It was very rock & roll. The only game in town for girls was getting fucked by one of Beuys' roadies. I don't think any women spoke.

In Essen, 1968, Thek staged his first gallery performance. When the pieces that he'd shipped from Rome arrived in Essen seriously damaged, he moved into the gallery and let the viewers watch while he repaired them. He called the show *A Procession in Honor of Aesthetic Progress.* Mike Kelley writes: "Thek exhibited sculptures damaged... in a gallery where they were bathed in pink light. In this light he worked on repairing them. When they were fixed, he moved them into a room lit with white light. They were reborn. They moved from the womb into the world."

Giuseppe and Pinocchio. Pink candles. Pyramids and

storks and bunnies. The Pied Piper of Hamlin creates a nation of enchanted children and leads them into a mass grave.

In Amsterdam in 1968, Thek resurrected the dead hippie as *The Fishman* – a wax sculpture of himself suspended in the air by ropes. He's Christ depicted as a deep sea diver. His arms are reaching upwards as he swims to free himself from a clinging school of phallic fish. When the Stedelijk invited him to do a show at Easter, he invited several of his friends to move into the museum with him... They called themselves *The Artist's Co-Op*. The piece, called *The Procession*, filled several rooms of the museum with *The Fishman*, a bunch of plaster dwarves, tables, chairs, old newspapers, a human-scale chicken coop with a table full of junk and Easter bunny eggs, a mirror, a live chicken. Much to the distress of the Dutch press, the artist borrowed several paintings by St. Vincent Van Gogh and hung them up around the mess. "Museo-masochism," one newspaper cried. Thek described the process: "It happens very quickly. Many people do many things. At a certain moment, it collides."

The only object still remaining from this show is an artist's book the Stedelijk published called *A Document*, by Thek and Edward Klein.

Ted Bonin, Paul Thek's current gallerist and dealer, let me see a copy of the book at his gallery in New York.

I made these notes:

"Wallpaper samples – *Artpress*, survey of contemporary art – Beuys Nauman de Maria – Animal postcards porn working photos living photos snapshots interiors – a harmonica – a few bottles of champagne – aerial view of ashtray – up against the background of the daily papers, sometimes magazines, a *New Yorker* article on "colleges."

Crow, snapshots of food, silk cord, a playing card, a shoelace, old family photos, tin foil, polaroids of all the artists, fish. Postcards of a giraffe. Reports from *Documenta*. Christo. Money, shotglasses –"

Thirty years later, the book functions like a time machine. As a work of art it's not "transcendent." Looking at it catapults you backwards to the particular reality of another era. Whoever made this book, it seemed, was living through a time where you can do no wrong, where every move's deliberate and hilarious, and everything you do is art. Each of its thirty pages represents a day, and each day, the cast of objects is re-arranged and photographed against the backdrop of a larger play, the world news as reported in the daily paper. The book's a blast because it makes anything seem possible. It is a medieval book of hours recast six centuries later in a place where no one seems to be in charge. Like theater, the work takes place in space and time. Reframe your life like it's a science lab and *anything that happens will be art*.

Pieces from *Procession* toured around America. Thek went to see the pyramids in Egypt, and then moved back briefly to New York to put up a show at Stable, and then the gallery closed. By 1970 he was back in Europe. He wrote: "My head is filled with sculptures + table-top dream environments – if only I had a place to build it all." Seeing a Robert Wilson play called *Deafman's Glance* in Paris, 1971, blew him away – the play was drawing from the same image-bank as Thek's *Processions* – there were the pyramids, the table-top, the makeshift house, a school of fish – according to Wilson's staging notes for *Deafman's Glance*, "Processions pass..." Famous for performances that lasted a minimum of several hours, Wilson's image-bank in *Deafman's Glance* was framed, tortuously and completely, by a sense of passing time. Like Kafka, who wanted to run away from Prague to join the Yiddish Traveling Theater, Thek must've seen the possibility that theater could be heaven. He went back to see it several times, eventually asking Wilson for a part. For the rest of the run in Paris, he performed.

Stockholm, 1971 – The Artist's Co-Op, this time numbering eight people, produces a piece called *Pyramid/A Work in Progress* at the Modern Art Museum. They live together, sometimes occupying the Museum. Thek writes in his diary:

> *Stockholm... tiny apt... Ann arrives – a week*
> *planning – smoking – cooking, eating, wine, opium,*
> *no showers. I on floor in hall... piles of stuff, building,*
> *building, noises, posters, painting autumn, island,*
> *1st snow pink, sleep in museum, guards, into prison,*
> *Bjorn, Sonja, public, boat, finding things, meeting*
> *spirits, old lady, queen, family man, Magic child, Edwin*
> *leaves, Toby leaves, Franz leaves, Michelle leaves...*
> *I remain.*

This time the environment is completely aboriginal. It includes a papier-mâché catacomb and tunnel, a salvaged sink, old bathtubs, some balsam pines. There are fast food containers, a scale model of a house, a washing-line with laundry hung to dry, a kitchen table cleared and lit for the arrival of visitors. Strapped underneath another table, *Fishman* hovers over everything, suspended from the ceiling. There are letters, postcards, drawings, nailed to the trees.

Thek's renamed dead hippie, by this time an old chestnut, lies in state beneath some sprouting tulip bulbs and onions in a packing crate. Museum visitors were recast as actors, walking along a dirt-packed route towards the "temple of time," a huge pyramid, past a shack called the "confessional."

It was impossible to view the piece without moving through an exploded Stations-of-the-Cross. To be inside the room was to become part of the procession. Because many of the Artist's Co-Op members were also visual artists, they contributed objects out of their own image-banks. Ann Wilson installed a breathtaking large sculpture called *Stag in the Boat*. She recalls imagining the piece while sitting on the beach at Fire Island and studying the work of Albert Ryder as three deer stepped forward from the dunes. Unlike many other "collaborations" of that era, *Pyramid* is extraordinary because it is a collaboration between equals, rather than the vision of one person enacted by his drones. But it's difficult to grasp the boundaries where the obsessions/dreams of every individual leave off. The objects are autonomous and yet *Pyramid/A Work In Progress* is nothing like a group show. It's more like a group mind.

Years later, Ann Wilson recalled that *Pyramid* was designed as a vehicle for self-exploration. Building a communal space that was large enough to hold them, they were assuming "self" could be discovered best while in a group. "The work," she wrote, "functioned as a sort of ritual that included the public." The environments were a social/spiritual metaphoric space that anyone might enter. "There was a general feeling," Wilson wrote "for the potential field of consciousness."

"I sometimes think," Thek told the writer Suzanne

Delahanty years later, "that there is nothing but time, that what you see and what you feel is what time looks like at that moment."

The choreographer Simone Forti discovered movement as a force that she could ride while tripping on mescaline with the people that she lived with in an abandoned farmhouse.

"We called ourselves Chia Jen, or The Family," Forti wrote in 1974. "The life we lived provided a matrix for the profuse visions we lived out in various twilights." Mostly, she experienced a curiously expanded, timeless sense of time, a sense she later translated into dance notation. "Flow was central to our system... To flow was to relinquish a great deal of control over who and what you were going to come in contact with. You did this by suspending all plans until each moment presented itself. One result was a very high level of coincidence. I came to think of coincidence as harmonic overtones of occurrence and twilight guideposts."

In Budapest and later in New York, Squat Theater sat "for hours, weeks, even months... throwing ideas around and finally discussing how a performance was going to happen, down to the most minute details – but never rehearsed," Eva Buchmiller and Anna Koos wrote years later.

"We were asked many times, why? It was a gut feeling. Certain actions were simply not fit to rehearse, like drawing blood from an arm, setting a smoke bomb on the street or having dinner onstage. We knew one another, trusted one another's range of possibilities, and considered one another's expressions to be authentic. There was no yardstick to measure individual achievement...In our performances we manifested an existence that overrode its representation," Koos and Buchmiller recalled.

WASHINGTON, DC, sometime in the late 1970s: a group of young white people in their early 20s walk single-file through the suburban neighborhood around the American University with their eyes closed, holding hands, following a swarthy man in his mid-40s. It's an exercise in "trust." Their leader wears a T-shirt and a Balinese sarong wrapped halfway round his pot belly. His name is Richard Schechner. At that moment, he is the director of The Performance Group in New York City; a tenured full professor at NYU, and the foremost theoretician on American experimental theater.

It's mid-July, and Richard wants us all to understand his dilemma. He recently came back from a Fulbright-funded trip to India and crashed into a mid-life crisis, the claustrophobia of fame, his job, his seven-room apartment. He spent the late Spring over-sleeping, dream-wracked, watching "the movies of his life." He told us he was hoping dreams could offer some career direction, impart some meaning, fill the void.

It's hard for us to relate first-hand to Richard's problems. When Richard was our age, he was already a professor at Tulane University and co-author of a book on the Free Southern Theater. The twelve of us support ourselves with part-time menial jobs. We've saved and borrowed, sold possessions to spend this month with him. Because we're hoping it will be an opportunity: that one of us will be the one to land an unpaid internship or a walk-on role in Richard's theater.

Our desperation bores him. He already has a full-time job; he only takes these summer stints as a means of giving paying work to actors in the Group. So instead of taking ordinary classes, he decides, we'll do a project, a group investigation into dreaming. Because at that time it seemed everyone believed the "self" is best discovered in a group. The twelve of us move from our dorm rooms into Richard's faculty apartment. We form a tribe. No one leaves without permission. We vow to live together, eat together, sleep together so that our dreams will merge into a slice of Jungian unconscious.

According to the books that Richard's studied, people dream most vividly during light and interrupted sleep. We agree to sleep in shifts so that we can wake each other before entering a state of full repose. We take turns being Sleep Monitors, armed with tape-recorders, pens and notebooks. Flashlights and alarm clocks become our most important tools.

Within days, we succeed in entering the cataleptic state of sleep-deprivation. And this works out really well, because Richard's also read that sleep deprivation was used in lieu of truth-drugs among Korean War prisoners. Eagerly we all agree to work with this. Because *things come out* when you're exhausted.

There is this rhetoric that everyone buys into about things *needing* to come out, as if the drug of choice were sodium pentathol. The whole concept's part New Age and part Rousseauian. As if, beneath the onion-skin of personalities, there lies the gleaming uncorrupted Human Soul.

As soon as our dreams have merged sufficiently we plan to stage them. But there's so much to do in four short weeks, yoga and plastiques and group dynamics, we never get around to this or any other acting. Therefore every moment of our collective life is experienced as part of the audition that Richard never holds.

Days begin on the American University football field at 6 a.m. with Induced Group Kundalini Vomiting. It's something Richard learned in India. To do it, you drink eight glasses of water really fast, then stick your index finger down your throat until you puke. Does Group Vomiting offer any avenues for career advancement? We try and make them. Who'll be bravest? Who'll be first? Who has the cleanest vomit?

Halfway through the workshop, a schizophrenic member of the group, Victoria, goes off her medication. She's hospitalized. We never hear from her again, and never ask. Her problems don't have much to do with us. Following the All Night Ghost Dance, several of us shared our individual beliefs that Richard appeared to be guiding the prettiest girl's hand beneath his Balinese sarong. Each of us was jealous. Still, each night in Gestalt Group Therapy, we compete for breakthroughs that will change our lives.

Franz Kafka wanted to join the Yiddish Traveling Theater because he thought that it could change his life. Theater, Kafka wrote, is heaven.

From Stockholm, Paul Thek wrote a postcard to Franz Decker: "The reviews were <u>fantastic</u>. Beyond belief… What next time will be, I don't know… but something else. Thicker. Deeper." "We were creating parables as fast as we could," Ann Wilson wrote much later.

In 1973 at *Documenta 5* the Artist's Co-Op mounted a huge installation called *Ark/Pyramid*. Rooms transformed into theatrical utopia. Like any kind of radical art, the Artist's Co-Op pieces redefine a genre. What is theater?

The Artist's Co-Op projects of the 1970s have wrongly been historicized as "scatter art" or "arte povera." In fact, the presence and the placement of what's strewn around these rooms is as intentional and charged as stage-props waiting to be animated by the actors, who will give them meaning (life).

In the theater world of the 1970s, the idea of "audience participation" was in vogue. Mostly this entailed the actors being touched by audience members, or town meeting-cum-group therapy debates about the outcome of the play. The Artist's Co-Op installations suggest it might be possible to have a play in which the *only* human actors are the spectators. In *Ark/Pyramid*, Ann Wilson's boat awaits entry through a drawbridge to an enormous pyramid built on raked-up tiers of sand. A bunny watches. It is Artaudian cruelty achieved by gentleness, a body without organs, a waking dream.

It's interesting to compare the Artist's Co-Op *Processions* of the 70s with contemporary installation art. Installation art implies a system. It's a machine, a thinking-process: objects and their associative links externalized. Is there a difference, then, between the kinds of systems made by one or many minds? Jennifer Stockholder's acclaimed *YourSkinInThis WeatherBourneEyeThreads&SwollenPerfume* (Dia, 1995) is a complex, highly fractured set of poetic-intellectual digressions and yet the objects ultimately fold back into themselves. However fractured, the installation is a single system.

Looking at the photos of the *Processions*, it's im-possible to systematize, what's happening. The field between the areas is so emotional and deep that even empty space assumes a contour. Subliminal cross-referencing, dense jungle cluster-fuck of objects. Is there any better picture of utopia? The *Processions* are ghost-theater: they are blatant, manifest and veiled.

"It's so – theatrical," is about the worst thing you can say about anybody's work in the contemporary artworld. Theatricality implies an embarrassing excess of presence, i.e., of sentiment. We like it better when the work is cool. Thek's work is often called "theatrical." I don't know if anybody else before or since has ever quite achieved what he accomplished in *Processions*: a degree-zero of theatricality, minus text and minus actors, achieved through purely visual means.

Imagine theater as a binary set of variables compressed within a time-based framework called "the play." Framed by time – that is, the time it takes the play to happen – theater is a series of synaptic intersections that occur between the actors and their characters, their props, the words they're speaking and their gestures. It's an emotional technology, a magic box. Even though the play's rehearsed and circum-scribed, the act of theater really happens in the tiny gaps between the actors and their roles, a friction witnessed by the audience, and all of this takes place within the confines of the "play."

In the *Processions*, objects take the place of actors. Crashpad living spaces anchored in a sea of sand. "Sand is water you can walk on, it's time," Thek said later. These objects have a history. Just as the entire rehearsal process is embedded in performance of each actor in a play, the objects in the *Procession* pieces vibrate with what brought them here. And yet they're porous, waiting to be filled by what happens next, their interaction with the audience. Because the only way of viewing any of the *Procession* installations is as an actor. The objects trigger thoughts, emotion, conversations. Some deadend and others intersect. The *Processions* borrow theater's finite sense of time – the Aristotelian image of a clock wound up and ticking – and expand it into a continuous present. The *Processions* shatter theater's fundamental limits by emotionally abstracting space and time.

LOS ANGELES, sometime in the late 90s –

I've been living here a year or two and the landscape is an empty screen of white sky days. There's nothing here except for what you're able to project onto it. No information, stimulation. No references, associations, promises and so your own reality expands to fill the day. It's freedom. I am an independent contractor of my own consciousness. Los Angeles is a triumph of the New Age. The only experience that comes close to totalizing effect of theater now is sadomasochism. It is utopian Diaspora. Because anyone who wants to can consent to play. It's portable, it's emotionally high-tech: the most time-efficient method of creating context and complicity between highly mobile units.

I am kneeling on the floor of the downstairs studio awaiting the arrival of a man I met over the telephone named Jason. A bowl of ice cubes sits melting on the wicker table. I am very nervous now about these ice cubes. Forty minutes ago, Jason called from Venice to say that he'd be leaving in 10 minutes. Jason tells me what to wear, what to do, what to say. Tonight's the first time that he's ordered ice cubes. It's a hot September night and Venice is about 22 miles away. It's difficult to time this right, because if I go downstairs too soon, the ice will melt completely, but Jason wants me kneeling, in position, the moment he walks in the door. My mind's already split in two: I'm halfway here, the other half of me is hovering above the 10 East freeway, following the likely progress of his car.

I've been kneeling here about 10 minutes in the sheer black blouse, the crotchless panties. I don't dare get up long enough to check my makeup. My back is straight, my palms and cunt are trembly. The motion-sensor light outside the house blinks on and then the door swings open. My eyes are lowered like he told me, looking only at the black jean legs below his waist. He shuts the door, I take the timing of his footstep as the cue to speak the line he gave me. My voice comes someplace from the swirl between my downcast eyes and the tension of his footstep, modesty and fear commingling like a cocktail of two complementary drugs, NOW – "My body is yours. You can do what you want with it." I'm speaking in a voice I've never used before.

There is no experimental theater in sadomasochism. That's why I like it. Character is completely preordained and circumscribed. You're either top or bottom. There isn't any room for innovation in these roles. And as you play them, something flips and you believe it. Balinese dance, Noh and Kathakali all use ancient gestures to create emotion. As the playwright and director Lee Breuer describes it, "the gestures reverse their way up through the stimulus system of the body, and go back into the ganglia and make emotion. It becomes a loop, and these loops together constitute the performing energy flow." The studded collar, wig and frilly see-through blouse tell me who to be and what to say. Tonalities and gestures are all completely set. His black Levis, my slutty outfit, his black shoes.

He says, *Get up. Yes sir*, I stumble. He clips my handcuffs to some device he's mounted on the door. *Legs spread. Hands against the wall. That's right.* He leaves me there, I feel him watching. This must be love because I feel myself expanding in his gaze and so I say *I want you to know I take this very seriously.* He listens, takes this in and slams an index finger up my pussy. *Heh heh. Just as I thought.* There are only two criteria for success within an s/m performance: wet or hard. And then his whip comes down across my back abrupt and sharp. *We'll start with ten. You'll count them off.* There's nothing sexual about this. The pain shakes through my back around the room and then there's two and three then – *Oooops. You forgot to thank me for them. We'll have to start again.*

S/m's another flip around the immanence of objects in the theater: the objects aren't blank and waiting to be filled by the presence of the actors and the play. The objects here are meaning-cards, they hold all the information. He puts a collar round my neck and slaps me. Handcuffs, blindfolds, gags and whips. Multiple paradox yielding triple penetration. The objects tell us who we are and what to do. S/m is like *commedia dell'arte,* a stock repertoire of stories, bits and lines and gags. We're Punch and Judy. He chains my handcuffs to the door. I'm Columbine and he's Pierrot.

YEARS LATER, Paul Thek's preoccupation with the character of time became more obsessive and explicit. The pyramid as a symbol of historical and sacred time. Paintings made on newspaper, the universal medium of temporality, "dramas and disasters that one day stun us and fade away the next." Holland Cotter, Thek's most astute and sympathetic critic, writes about the artist in the early 70s in Rome, "passing day after day in fluid, memoryless drug time – 'chemical vacations' – cruising monuments and bridges and baths seeking time-suspending sexual encounters."

Ironically, Thek had this in common with his enemies, the minimalists. In 1966, the artist Robert Smithson described his friend Dan Flavin's monuments as objects in which "both past and future are placed into an objective present... Time breaks down into many times... A million years is contained in a second..." (*New Entropy*)

Living alone in New York City in the early 1980s, Thek was thinking about joining a Benedictine monastery. He wasn't drawing much. Instead he kept a diary. Around that time he wrote: "My work is about time. An inevitable impurity from which we all suffer." The stand-out painting from Thek's final show before his death of AIDS in 1988 was the image of a clock surrounded by the words the *face of GOD*. I don't think the poignancy of this is diminished by its obviousness.

Time was the not-so-secret weapon of the medieval church; the tolling of the church bells every quarter hour was a ubiquitous reminder of Death-the-Universal-Leveler. In the early centuries of the first millennium, the Gnostics believed that the souls of dead people entered the earth's atmosphere as pure *information*. It was like the first sci-fi technology of time-travel. The living can absorb the dead at any time. Therefore everyone knows everything and all time exists simultaneously. The species has an infinite capacity for memory. Time is mixed with blood. At the end of the French Revolution's reign of terror in 1789, the Jacobins invented a new calendar. The revolution is a break with past recorded time, ushering in a new regime. The years had names: Humidor and Thermador. Pol Pot, who'd studied history at the Sorbonne, tried to do this too after murdering half the population of Cambodia. Time starts new. In the 1920s, the Dadaist Hugo Ball saw his nomadic movements around the backwater towns of Europe as a flight out of time. He wanted to arrive someplace where time stood still. Is it a coincidence that Ball, like Thek and Simone Weil, was ambivalently Catholic?

The Artist's Co-Op dissolved sometime in the mid 70s, though how it happened isn't documented. Endings of utopias hardly ever are. Holland Cotter describes Paul Thek alone in Italy in 1975 "waiting for mail that never arrives, brooding on unsettled scores and missed opportunities, unable to motivate himself to exercise, much less to make art, too bored to stay but too frightened to leave." Around that time, Thek wrote in his diary:

> My head begins to open, open. Praise the
> Lord. I see the completion of the Pied Piper's
> blanket. I will go to the foundry tomorrow.
> All day I try to keep with God. It is better.
> I keep on center, neutral. Praise the Lord.
> No hashish. I see the importance of withdrawing
> from sex in order to make the progress I wish.
> Too easily distracted... I see how important it
> is for me to AVOID HASHISH...

When the Lucerne Art Museum declined, in 1976, to continue storing Ark/Pyramid, the largest of the Artist's Co-Op pieces, it was destroyed.

In 1977, the critic-curator Suzanne Delahanty staged a retrospective of Thek's work at the ICA in Philadelphia. Eagerly, Thek moved back to New York. He thought this show would reinsert him in the New York artworld where he'd been absent for a decade. He hoped the show would move the Artist's Co-Op projects from the European counter-culture to a place within the context of art history but nothing really happened. The show hardly got reviewed. Thek blamed it on the curator.

After the show stayed in New York City, writing to his friend Franz Deckwitz:

> *Things are quite bad for me now, I live on*
> *borrowed $ and only occasionally do I manage*
> *to sell something. You see I was out of this*
> *country for too long and now mostly they have*
> *new people and things are difficult even for*
> *them. America is very competitive you know,*
> *always changing, and it was not wise for me*
> *to spend so much time away from my home,*
> *time has come and gone for me it is a bit like*
> *starting over again… I have taken a job here*
> *in a supermarket.*

The ex-Warhol Factory actress Penny Arcade dropped into a performance evening at the St. Marks Poetry Project in New York City in 1981. She'd been out of New York City for a decade, living on a Greek island with some poets, running a theater group in rural Maine. That night she felt like Rip Van Winkle. Everything had changed. A couple of poker-faced white guys who'd just got out of Dartmouth stood up reciting facts they'd learned about the pointlessness of language. A summary of their credentials, grants, awards, filled the entire printed program. They were ridiculous. Everyone took them seriously. The performance wasn't funny. In Penny's ethos the greatest artists were contemptuous of the entire notion of career. It was a coercive lie. Living an artistic life meant doing anything you want to do, and people got on stage to entertain and *do something*.

By the late 1970s the Artist's Co-Op seemed anachronistic, Holland Cotter explains, trying to translate Paul Thek's dilemma, because "painting had come back in a big way... and with that, a renewed esteem for the solid, purchasable object." By the mid 1980s, Thek was in New York and making paintings once again. But they were small and bright and full of religious sentiment and by that time the fashion of the day was dark and raw heroic neo-Expressionism...

Six weeks later Penny's rage exploded in her first original performance. Paul Thek and Penny never met but later on their histories crossed. When the photographer Shayla Baykal, an original member of the Artist's Co-Op died leaving Penny as her executor, she left behind some notebooks, remnants of the now-dispersed *Processions*. Two of Thek's magnificent last paintings inherited from Baykal now hang in Penny's loft above the ashes of the late Jack Smith whose estate Arcade also manages.

Living in New York during the late 1970s Thek was justifiably bitter. His career trajectory had run from controversial art star to supermarket worker over the past decade. In his diary he sardonically observes:

"NOW + THEN it occurs to me that I really LIKE my life, my life as BAD EXAMPLE..."

"How does the relationship of the French Situationists to their culture compare to the Yippie's relationship to American culture?" Mike Kelley asks in *Death and Transfiguration*. "You'll never know. Because all the Americans among this group have been categorized as hippies, not artists. They don't count. ...Death of a hippie? How can something die that was born dead."

I have to keep reminding myself that Thek was not a parable, he was a person. Because after all to see him as a martyr is to play into art history's hand. Broke and moving between provincial backwaters, making enemies at every turn, the Dadaist Hugo Ball interpreted his life as parable. Ball fervently believed his restless life embodied all the dissonances of his age. But it's difficult not to see Paul Thek as some kind of misplaced modernist, channeling unhappiness like information from the culture, because the unhappiness reflected in his diary when he moved back to New York during the 1970s was just so huge.

Paul Thek died bitterly in New York of AIDS in that most bitter Year of Our Lord 1988, the year described by Eileen Myles in *A Poem* when –

> *We realize the city was*
> *sold in 1978.*
> *But we were asleep.*
> *We woke and the victors*
> *were all around us,*
> *criticizing our pull-chain lights*

And we began to pray.

When an uncontainable artist's influence won't go away, art history compromises by constructing hagiographies. At least that way the vision is contained. But you have to keep reminding yourself of the great dead artist's situation. That he also had contemporaries. That thoughts are never thought alone.

I am trying to locate Paul Thek when he was unhappy in New York in 1979. Thek was close friends with the photographer Peter Hujar, who lived on Second Avenue before he died in 1987. Hujar was close friends with David Wojnarowicz who also lived on Second Avenue for many years. David was still a teenage hustler from New Jersey working around the bars on 42nd Street and the West Side piers when he met Peter Hujar. And even though by then Hujar had renounced the artworld, turned his back on a career, he made David think it might be interesting and possible to be an artist. This according to the hagiography of David Wojnarowicz. Like all hagiographies, the facts are probably mostly true, minus all the doubts and boredom that surrounded them in real time.

In 1979 I was living on Second Avenue in the East Village. My best friend Debbie Pinto shared a place with Bess and Ricky on East 9th. Debbie ended up in New York City after working as a barker in a carnival. She'd run away from home in a trailer park in Michigan at age 14. Debbie grew up singing country & western. She wrote songs and played guitar and she and Bess, a bass player, had a band. They worked as paper-girls and sold amphetamine.

One night Debbie was depressed and we made a plan that

she'd come meet me after work when the topless bar where I was working closed. Probably Deb was speeding because she walked all the way uptown. Around Times Square she started talking to some guy who offered her a taste of uncut crystal meth. So Debbie followed him to his hotel room upstairs but before they even did a line, he locked the door and punched her in the eye. He was a pimp. He tied her to the bed. Deb was carrying an address book and he promised that he'd kill her and several of her friends if she ever ran away or told the cops or anybody else. His whores walked in and out. When Debbie finally stopped struggling he taught her how to give a blowjob, gave her a wig, a pair of goggle sunglasses and a dress and turned her out. Five days later, a nice trick in a Buick from New Jersey drove her back downtown. Shortly after, Deb got married to a Christian, was born again and moved to a mining town in England. Her life doesn't lend itself so well to hagiography.

> *This morning I got up and I barely*
> *knew where I was, I walked*
> *around naked for awhile, checking*
> *out my identity in the long*
> *mirror in the front room & I*
> *was disappointed in what I saw,*
> *humiliated by time, and*
> *accident, and now the cup*
> *passing me by… again.*
> *So I walked around naked awhile,*
> *checking it out, a big city sky,*
> *all Dec. grays & fog, outside a*
> *rickety NY tenement window,*

outside the dirty dirty window, the dirty dirty
storm window, the city & the
city sky… & inside. ?me, & late.
getting up morning & walking around naked
checking my identity, checking my
physicality, sly suspicious glances in the mirror, afraid
to look close, and then I shower.

– Paul Thek diary, November 7, 1979

I don't know where Paul Thek was living but I associate this writing with a movie, *Queer and Alone* by Jim Strahs and Ken Kobland. The entire film consists of just one take, one shot: a guy sitting two floors above the Bowery in a straight-backed chair beside a window. His accent says he comes from someplace else. That he's some kind of factory worker, carnival roustabout or drifter who's outlived his time.

So maybe Paul Thek's room was on the Bowery, or maybe farther down on Church Street, which was then a transitional zone of low-end offices: back-office data processors, sole proprietor wholesale jewelers, replaced by bootleg artist's lofts and studios as the businesses failed or people died. A guy looks out his window and it's empty. Mornings rumbling that November around eight or nine: bike messengers weaving around garbage trucks, the morning drunks lined up outside McCanns, the rush of people climbing up the subway stairs to grab a takeout coffee before going to their jobs.

And then I take a long shower, a
long long shower, crummy tenement
tiny bathroom, everything peeling

paint & cracks, a long shower

in a messy bathroom. The
physical identity that I'd been
checking out in the mirror stands a long
long while under the hot shower & praises
God & tries to clear its mind, and
lets God clear its mind & goes to
God

he occupied himself, for lack of
decent company, with the
writing of endless "journals"

At 9 a.m. that November morning I was probably in that street en route to some awful typing job but now I'm in the room with him behind the dirty window. Reading this I realize I can hardly picture him at all.

The hardest thing to picture is what it's like to live inside a body that is male. Thinning hair and hollow chest, a belly spilling over jeans? A body, isolated in the box of this apartment. It hits the walls and bounces up against the boredom of diminished expectations. Why is it that a man alone inside a room always seems so much more alone than a woman? Imagining it now, trying to pour pieces of myself into this other person's body, feels so contained and trapped. A body, muscular and soft and tense against the heavy molecules of air around it. Queer and alone, sex-soul-energy throbbing up against the boundaries of his skin –

I bring Thek's diaries to my writing class. "There is no way," the girls all say, "that we can identify with this. When someone goes this far out, they aren't letting anybody in." But why does writing need to do this? In her introduction to Thek's diaries, Rebecca Quaytman notes that like his paintings, they are disarmingly devoid of artistry. As Thek once said about his early sculptures, "They are agnostic. They lead nowhere, except perhaps to a kind of freedom."

Thek longed to join a Carthusian monastery in Vermont during the last years of his life. He never did. *At times there was sun, and then shadow again.*

He wrote to the brothers in Vermont: "I've traveled too much and too long to have been absorbed into any community. I came to a kind of reawakening only rather late in life and have felt a fish out of water ever since... I already spend far more time actually alone than any of you do and I have no sharing community to return to when my aloneness becomes too great... Perhaps my own creative work might be continued there?"

96 Sacraments, a text Thek wrote in Europe, is a heart-breaking and inspiring record of a person's effort to transcend boredom and invest daily life with weight. To experience both gravity and grace.

> *To go out. Praise the Lord.*
> *To see the sun. Praise the Lord.*
> *To do the shopping.*
> *To mail a letter. Praise the Lord.*
> *To talk with some people.*
> *To buy a paper.*
> *To come home.*
> *To go to work.*
> *To work.*

> *To have lunch. Sing Praises!*
> *To notice the light changing. Sing Praises*
> *To see a cat. Praise the Lord Sing Praises*

Belief is a technology, a mental trick for softening the landscape. The world becomes more sensuous and beautiful when God is in it.

> *The hymn died away – Lenz spoke. He was shy. During the singing his numbness had completely disappeared… A sweet feeling of endless well-being came over him.*

Simone Weil wrote about the way she tried "to see a landscape as it is when I'm not there… What do the energy, the gifts etc. that are in me matter? …If only I knew how to disappear there'd be a perfect union of love between God and the earth I tread, the sea I hear." Sometimes I try this in Los Angeles.

Thek's last paintings are often criticized for being too "precious" and too "pretty." He installed a show of them so low, in 1988, that people had to sit in children's chairs to see them. Later, Thek's career was described by Richard Flood, who he'd long since made an enemy of, as "one of the great failures in contemporary art."

> "Why Am I So Boring." *11-7-79*
> *Thank God the past is over!*
> *Wondering why I feel so*
> *bored, so unattached, un*
> *dedicated, why my best*
> *energies and attitude, best*

actions are for some reason
unused, undone, etc., perhaps
it's because my "real" responsibility
is being avoided, denied,
almost ridiculed... i.e. painting?
or rather women? or ptgs of them?
Things growing are not ripe until
their season.
"The Prodigal Prodigy"
Things growing are not ripe until
their season.

Time is all that anyone is ever left with. There's nothing "pretty" about the diaries Thek was writing. Reading them that Friday evening in Berlin made me understand that writing can be bad and still be part of something good. That "art" is really "artifact," Exhibit A, Exhibit B, of something else: a person's whole experience and life. And that always there is the chance that this will fail. That things will *not* work out.

3.

Gravity & Grace: Production – Easton, Pennsylvania, Auckland, New Zealand, New York City 1993–1994

SYLVERE AND I spent the Fall of 1992 hiding out in Easton, Pennsylvania, a forgotten town about 60 miles west of New York City, with Lily, our dachshund-cocker spaniel. Rents were cheap and I was due to leave the country for New Zealand to start working on the film in early January. So instead of reclaiming our New York apartment, or our East Hampton house, or our farmhouse in the upstate town of Thurman which all were profitably rented, we packed up the car and moved again. Since that February, I'd been on tender-hooks with New Zealand, trying to raise the money for the film. In July the funding finally came through. Moving seemed like an adventure.

All year we'd been on a pilgrimage in search of money. While Sylvère, a Columbia University professor, had a considerable reputation and career, I hadn't had an opportunity in ten years. Since 1982 I'd been a "filmmaker," producing dense and difficult, unlikeable experimental movies, exhibiting them in clubs and venues where projectors broke and people talked and heckled. By then I'd nearly given up, spending months up in our farmhouse volunteering at the local school, making mustard pickle and contemplating suicide while Sylvère wrote his lectures.

It was unthinkable that anyone would ever help me make a feature in New York. So that year, I hatched a final plan: to go back to New Zealand as if finishing a successful ten-year sojourn and look for money there. Luckily, my ambitions meshed with Helen Benneham's. Helen, who at that time was head of a well-funded art organization, was very interested in my background. She'd been seeking ways to forge connections between the Auckland art world and New York, and wasn't it true that I was married to Sylvère Lotringer, the critic?

Clumsily, we made a deal. If I could write something that looked like a "short drama," she'd push my application through for $40,000. In exchange, Sylvère would come while I was there to lecture and maybe do a project with some local artists. Helen couldn't pay for an entire feature, but if I raised funds to shoot the last half of the movie in New York with the New Zealand cast and crew, she'd "find a way" for us to finish.

Sylvère and I agreed it was the best offer I'd had from anyone in a decade. We knew that making *Gravity & Grace* would be expensive, so that year we agreed to rent everything we owned and go anywhere where people paid us.

As soon as Sylvère's classes finished that May, we went from New York to Los Angeles; then to Berlin to make $4,000; back to Los Angeles and then to Riparius, New York, where we'd found a two-room shack to rent for August in order not to disrupt the rental of our ten-room farmhouse.

When the lease ran out on Labor Day we loaded up the Ford Granada with all our traveling stuff and furniture. Lily squeezed her bonsai-body in between the futon mattress, books and thrift-store crockery. We didn't know exactly where we'd land but our vague plan was to drive south until we found a quaint exurban slum with cheap apartments and bus service to New York.

Easton fitted that description perfectly. We got there when the sun was going down, about 6:30. And partly we didn't want to hassle with the carload full of stuff or spend another 50 bucks for a motel, and partly it was the ghost-town atmosphere that lured us, the cobbled streets, the already crumbling faces of the 18th century buildings that were last restored during the Jimmy Carter 70s. We bought a local paper and within three hours, signed the lease to a $600 p/month townhouse.

All Fall we lived at 620 Front Street like terrorists shunted between safehouses. It didn't take us long to learn the town. Our house was opposite the Municipal Town Center. Two blocks down where Front crossed Main there was a diner, several thrift stores, and an old-style ticket office-waiting room for the Transbridge Bus to New York City. Three blocks east there was an iron girder bridge over the Delaware River that separated Easton from New Jersey. *America Starts Here* the road-sign sighed. Further into town, there was a tattoo parlor and a cheese store and several hair salons. There was a crayon factory and foundry and several old abandoned mills. I couldn't ever get a grip on what this part of Pennsylvania was and it never occurred to Sylvère to even try.

Sylvère set his office in the middle room downstairs on the second floor. From the big bay window he could see the gray slate roofs and turrets of the other houses reaching up towards College Hill. It was a bit like Philadelphia, a bit like France. Sylvère was working on an essay on the sacred sociologists Henri Michaux and Georges Bataille. It didn't really matter where he was. One day a pale Jehovah's Witness and his son came knocking on the door. He let them in and put them in the essay too.

Every quarter hour the town clock on the Municipal

Center Tower chimed. I was sitting in my office working on the script, pretending Easton was a medieval town. *Every fifteen minutes brings us closer to our deaths, the day of reckoning.* Mostly Lily slept, curled up neatly underneath the makeshift table. At 14, with rheumy eyes and graying hair around her muzzle she was already getting old.

A retired bookkeeper named Mary Schumaker lived in the small ground floor apartment underneath us. Her room was filled with clocks and crocheted comforters. She'd been in Easton all her life.

Late afternoons, Sylvère and I took Lily for a walk along the towpath by the river. A century ago or maybe two, men and animals had pulled barges through it down the river. It was possible, the bookkeeper told us, to walk all the way to Philadelphia, fifty miles.

Late afternoons the sky was full of birds. Enormous migratory formations of barn swallows began arriving as the leaves were turning and they stayed until the trees were bare. When the leaves were gone, the swallows filled the branches like round oranges or apples. Time moved forward. The real America, cars and malls and condominiums, started on the edge of Easton, so we just stood still.

Tuesdays and Thursdays Sylvère drove in to teach his classes in the city. Mostly he looked forward to the ride back home. He'd found a radio station playing late night jazz from Newark. He was 56 years old.

Sylvère was thinking constantly about his childhood in the countryside near Paris in the war years, 1941–1944. His friend Denis Hollier had written a poetic essay about the philosopher Georges Bataille during those years, and Sylvère was haunted by a phrase that Denis used: "the smell of wartime." It was a phrase so lyrical and pure, evoking gaslit streets and gentle rain, gabardine and cobblestones, a thawing rutabaga field. Sylvère, a European Jew, who spent the war years hiding in a farm behind that field, experienced "the smell of war-time" as a stench, numb terror. It was a numbness that he'd carried deep inside himself for fifty years. One Sunday driving north along the river we came upon an abandoned quarry and a mill.

Re-reading *Gravity and Grace* by Simone Weil, I identified with the dead philosopher completely. Like her, I had a chronic illness that often made it difficult to eat. Both of us had long necks and shoulders that hunched forward when we walked, a clumsy eagerness that tried against all odds to break outside the limits of our awkward bodies. We both smoked handrolled cigarettes and had absolutely zero sense of our own "femininity" or gender. We'd both been ridiculed at school, and later too, in the eternal high-school of the artworld.

Sylvère-the-pragmatist kept telling me I'd have better luck if I'd just call myself a "feminist" but I just couldn't do it. Because I'd been sad so long I could not believe in merely personal salvation, and anyway the feminists we knew were mostly Good Girl Academics. Why should women settle to think and talk about just femaleness when men were constantly transcending gender?

"Just because things seem serious," the Perfect Guy tells Gravity in a bar, "doesn't mean they really are."

All that Fall in Easton, Sylvère and I moved haphazardly through an improvised routine that on the face of it looked normal. We cooked meals, ran errands, worked in our two offices, took walks along the towpath, joined a gym. But this domestic life was like a finger holding back a flood because really everything was crumbling.

That September, the lawyer for the consortium that owned our Second Avenue apartment tracked us down to serve a notice of eviction. Our friend Maija who'd been living there had apparently signed a deposition.

In October, the tiny lump we'd had removed from Lily's breast two years ago returned suddenly, only this time it was huge.

In November, there were New York events to celebrate the publication of two books our company had published. And even though I'd edited the books, I was resented all the time it took. I'd waited, what, ten years to make this movie? I was running out of time and couldn't bear the thought of spending one more month promoting other people's work. All year I'd been channeling a book by my friend, the poet David Rattray. I asked him questions and he wrote the answers. No matter where I was, David phoned me every day and I listened to him talk for sometimes hours. I loved his book and now that it was finally coming out, I couldn't understand why David didn't seem the least bit interested in my movie. He'd even written about Simone, called her the counterpart of Nietzsche. Weeks passed before he had the chance to read my script, and when he did, he merely commented on one or two misspellings.

We took Lily to a vet on College Hill and when the biopsy came back, she determined that the tumor was malignant. Her twelve pound body shrank; she shivered. We cooked her special meals to coax her appetite and bought her a cableknit wool sweater. By December, Sylvère carried her inside his coat when we took our walks. We set her down among the leaves to smell the ground beside the towpath.

That same month David posted me a crazy letter. He'd done a reading from his book at a bar on Avenue B where people heckled and *could no longer see the point* in participating in a culture that was *completely bankrupt and degenerate*. Two days later he collapsed on Avenue A with a massive brain tumor—

We visited him that week at St. Vincent's Hospital. His eyes seemed very large. His face was gaunt and wrapped up in gauze bandages. The tumor, as they'd thought, was much too large to be removed with surgery. David, we'd thought, with his patrician background and full medical insurance, would've been a perfect candidate for experimental high-tech treatments at Sloane Kettering or in Switzerland or Paris but he rejected this. David was quite content to stay on at St. Vincent's. The ward oncologist was a Pakistani reader of the Islamic poetry David had been translating; they swapped epigrams in Arabic.

David explained to me that he'd be dying very soon. He was speaking in a voice that was both inside and distanced from his terror. We'd talked often about the notion of "the good death" that had prevailed in western culture through the 19th century; now he was having one. The poet-doctor sent him home to rest before a perfunctory round of chemotherapy.

I went to visit David at his Avenue A apartment on the way to catch the plane to Auckland. They'd just moved him from the hospital and his wife Lin Rattray asked if I could run out to buy some pillows. The plane was leaving in three hours and I ran and caught a cab downtown and shopped and ran some more and burst into the fourth-floor walk-up, sweating.

David smiled wanly, "Chris, you're a brick," and then I

left to catch the plane.

> *Who are we*
> *We are no one*
> *What do we want*
> *A human head*

> *Who are we*
> *We are everyone*
> *What do we want*
> *A large portable fan*
> *And an aeroplane*

> *So we can go*
> *Zoom golly golly golly*
> *Zoom golly golly*
> *Zoom golly golly golly*
> *Zoom golly golly*

> *Life takes off like a jet!*

> – Barbara Barg, *After Agriculture*
> performed in *Gravity & Grace*

THIRTY HOURS later I arrived in Auckland. It was January 8, the height of New Zealand summer. Helen Benneham was on vacation, so right away before the jetlag even settled I called up Chev Murphy. Chev was my oldest closest New Zealand friend, and as always, Chev was around. Chev was one of those rare people who when you meet, you start up a conversation that you know will last a lifetime. We'd been on-and-off in love for nearly twenty years over several different cities. And while Sylvère's image of the gap-toothed chronically underemployed autodidactic grifter was considerably less rosy, Sylvère was pleased that Chev was there. I'd have somebody to talk to. This visit, Chev was on the dole. He had lots of time, no money. So we agreed, if I could pay, we'd drive out together to the beach for several days.

Have I mentioned I was very frightened? I got off the plane with nothing but Helen Benneham's grant letter and a script and in four months had to somehow shoot a movie. I hadn't lived here for a decade and had no contacts, no producer. Often I got sick with Crohn's Disease and while Sylvère was wonderful at taking care of me and keeping me out of the hospital, what if it happened here? There was a vague plan that Chev would be the bodyguard, the spiritual advisor.

Chev was a professional enthusiast. I've never known anyone capable of receiving so much pleasure from a book or song or jacket. Chev had installed a shrine on the wall of his Grey Lynn bedsit to his current female heroes. He even had a picture of Simone.

In his 20s, Chev had been a simple hippie, living in a part of London called The Angel and swallowing hallucinogens for months on end with his gorgeous English girlfriend. She'd even followed him back to Wellington, but when she left him, Chev's perceptions hardened. His two best friends from Hamilton Boys' High were now leaders in the Revolutionary Worker's Party. Unlike the hippie-student left, the RWP was a serious organization, with links, it was rumored, to Albania.

Hank and Martin, a labor organizer and a poet, undertook their old friend Chev's reeducation and he excelled. Unlike them, he was a genuine lumpen-prole. He'd left Hamilton Boys' High to go to work at age 15, his Dad was a casual day-laborer. And yet Chev read more than anyone at university. Politics gave Chev's intellectual curiosity a focus. He read Lenin, Marx and Habermaas. "If it was written by a human being, then it must be possible for another human being to understand it," he'd say with a radiant and prematurely toothless smile.

Around the time of Lech Walesa, the New Zealand Revolutionary Worker's Party fell apart. Like all the other communists, Hank and Martin fled back to the demands of their young families and professions. Chev, who had no family or career, only half recanted. He shifted his allegiances to the Trots, who'd always been less puritanical than the RWP, embracing gay and lesbian issues and cultural politics. That year Chev marched at the front of the Gay Rights March carrying a banner. He decided he was gay. Later after some consideration he amended this position to bisexual. Sneered at by straights and gays alike, bisexuality presented many opportunities for activism.

I'd visited Chev three years ago in a Socialist Action commune. He and five other comrades were working shifts at a cardboard box factory and a sausage plant. The Auckland chapter had decided to combat Socialist Action's insularity by leaving their cheap and cozy Victorian flats near the university and renting a tract house some fifteen miles south an industrial suburb, Otahuhu. Chev had been placed in charge of the First Annual Trotskyite Otahuhu Pig Roast. He was truly happy. Two years before that, when Chev was back in London working as a porter, we'd had a passionate affair and promised each other never to grow up, i.e., become like Hank and Martin.

But everything seemed different this time around. The SAL disbanded sometime after the Berlin Wall came down in '92. Chev was 45 and there was suddenly no glamour to being single and serially employed at shit jobs, without any credentials or marketable skill. Chev was so gregarious, the consummate communard. He'd always been a part of something. That afternoon, while we were riding in the car, he told me about some people who he'd met that were running therapy encounters aimed at altering the behavior of convicted sex offenders. They had offices and weekly groups and ran weekend marathons where they helped each other to a point where *things came out*. Chev was so impressed by the warmth and structure of the group that he started to remember things... the attraction that he'd felt to his ex-girlfriend's daughter, a child of just 13. He was a pervert, too! Because this attraction was entirely unconsummated, this confession didn't lead to jail. Instead, it was a ticket into a therapeutic subculture of confrontation groups and self-help teams where he found he could excel.

Unlike the educated leftists, the pervert-therapists took an interest in Chev's future. They sent him out on courses and paid for him to teach while he was training to be certified. They were grooming him for a professional career within the movement. Chev earnestly explained that he traced his deviancy to a sexual encounter with a cousin in his teens. It was a recovered memory.

I listened, pleased for him and disappointed. We were no longer playing Chicken. Since remaining adolescent means rejecting all compensatory lies about one's life, I knew the bet was off.

SYLVERE'S MONEY paid for the motel. In April when I finally did get sick and was hooked up to an IV at Auckland General, Delphine and Chev were busy watching videos together, but that came later. That January at the beach, we hung around and read and went for walks and both agreed without discussing it to cut the visit short.

So yes, by that time things were adding up to one of those moments where you can no longer count on any of the mythologies you've believed in and you don't have any new ones to replace them. Things don't come out. They fall apart.

4.

"It's time we thought about leaving the body behind."
William Burroughs & Brion Gysin, *The Third Mind*

SNAPSHOT OF this moment (Friday, November 20, East Hampton, 1998) – Sylvère and I are Bouvard and Pecuchet. It is a relatively mild light gray November day. Brown leaves come down. Piles of leaves along the road waiting to be collected by the town. High tide. Stalks of ragweed along the shore still green and yellow – they look unusually juiced and jungly up against the dying grass and bay. I am sitting on the O'Tooles' back deck along the water on Squaw Road – the street where Sylvère and I lived on and off for several years. Last year the house was sold. For several weeks I was absorbed in what I was writing. Now I'm not so sure –

I got here from LA on September 1, about 10 weeks ago. Took a semester off from school. Have started reading a book called *Sir Vidia's Shadow* by Paul Theroux, about his friendship with another writer, V.S. Naipul. I started reading it because it came up in conversation recently with Gavin Brice, the person I've been having long-distance sadomasochistic phone sex with since September 3. Gavin's a successful film producer. This fact struck me as ironic when we "met" about ten weeks ago at midnight on the LA Telepersonals Chat Line, and I told him how I'd come out here to write about the failure of my pathetic independent film. Gavin laughed. He was calling from North Africa. He had about a thousand people working for him, and they were about to start production on a mid-budget Hollywood film.

It was my third night staying in my husband's girlfriend's house on Seacrest Lane. Both of them were in New York, a hundred miles away. Because I spent a lot of time alone back in LA, calling the Telepersonals had turned into a habit. Before I went to sleep, or when I took a break from work, or on long stretches of hot afternoons alone I liked to listen to the sounds of people's voices on the Domination and Submission phone sex line. It was a loose network of the workaholic self-employed. Sometimes we traded messages about the things we'd do. No one in the artworld that I knew was interested in domination and submission, or even ordinary sex. S/m was a practicable skill. Sometimes the messages led to an exchange of actual phone numbers, and sometimes these conversations led to meetings. The messages gave me something to look forward to. Whereas in New York, having sadomasochistic sex in cars with strangers was something I would never do, in Los Angeles it was a pleasant vacation from a life that was superficially demanding but never entirely absorbing. Things happened but they never added up, there were countless conversations but no exchange of information, that moment when you feel your words and gestures enter someone else's field. Playing s/m with strangers made me feel that there was someone I was talking to.

Back in New York there were real things and conversations, landscape, history, people, houses, things to want and envy, so I never would've called the LA Telepersonals if I hadn't spent the past three days settling in Roberta's house, dismantling the shrine she'd set up on the downstairs bookcase, a drawing of my husband's penis surrounded by pieces of linoleum she'd salvaged from the house we'd lived in on Squaw Road. "But Chris, she is an artist," he'd rationalized. And then there was the phone call with my friend-enemy Danielle, Voice of the Super-Ego from Manhattan, who even without hearing about the penis shrine wondered what aspect of my damaged childhood had led me to accept a situation that seemed so fraught and compromised. Danielle talked about her therapist, her agent, her Mature Relationships and I hung up forty minutes later feeling like a cockroach, wishing something fabulous would happen, and then it did.

For the first time ever, from the safety of 3,000 miles, I called the LA Telepersonals Chatline and went on live as *Karen, a submissive woman who wants to play with a dominant guy who knows what he's doing and why he's doing it,* and at that moment Gavin Brice was lying on his studio-compound king-size bed some 14,000 miles away, sampling female voices and pressing the number 3 for "next." Gavin picked right up on "Karen" because very few live messages say anything about s/m. He left some messages and said he liked my voice, it sounded strong. And as everybody knows the game is better when the sub has something to exchange.

We traded messages back and forth, flirting, joking, dropping little bits of information that might distinguish us from all the other "Gavins," "Karens," on the line. Finally around midnight we connected live. Gavin had the foreign accent of someone who has moved around a lot. It sounded English, but then again it could have been Australian or South African. I remember telling him how my marriage sounded strange to most Americans. "Oh," he said, "then where're you from?" And when I told him Wellington, New Zealand he confessed to having spent a decade there. Not only was Gavin Brice a film producer, he'd lived within a half a mile of me. Everyone in New Zealand is a kind of cousin.

We'd known the same local personalities, gone to the same pubs and parties. I'd reviewed one of his early films, a classic, for the local paper, had hung around with many of his friends and though he was no longer so connected to New Zealand in the 90s, he said he'd heard about my film.

The confluence of everything that night was fabulous. Gavin had traveled extensively. Not only did we share these references to provincial grunge, when I told him all about the house on Seacrest Lane, he knew exactly where it was. Gavin adores the Hamptons. He tells me he's a friend of Claudia Schiffer, who owns a house here in the Hamptons, as well as Paul Theroux. For all I know Gavin might also know Chev Murphy, though as yet I haven't asked him. It's no coincidence that we're both attracted to s/m because we both crave glamour, which we define, like Gavin's favorite writer Joseph Conrad, as that moment when you're standing on a cliff not knowing what will happen next, about to jump: that "absolutely pure, uncalculating, unpractical spirit of adventure…"

That night we talked about an hour and I gave Gavin my real phone number and now I never know when he will call, though usually when he does it's around 11 in North Africa. There is a time difference of eight hours and unconsciously I time my walks.

Gavin's reading tastes intrigue me. He likes the classics. After spending 18 hours in the office, on the set or on the phone he sits up reading late at night. Sometimes when we aren't telling stories to get each other off e.g. – *I'm on the carphone on the LIE… I'm coming out to see you from New York* – he talks to me about his favorite writers, Shakespeare, Joseph Conrad, Robert Stone. In this book I'm reading now that Gavin recommended, Paul Theroux recounts advice once given him by Naipul, ten years the elder: "The greatest writing is a disturbing vision offered from a position of strength." And as I read this, it occurs to me that this is *exactly* what I dislike most about the classics, i.e., Great Male Writing. It's like Andre Breton boasting once to his Surrealist cronies about how he'll never let a woman see him naked unless his dick is hard –

Gavin keeps a running tally of his phone bill. So far he's spent about $500 on these calls. Since money is the medium of his profession, this fact does not particularly impress me. Still, each time he calls, I reciprocate by writing him a pornographic email and then he calls again so we can act out the next installment on the phone. It occurs to me, by doing this it might be possible to learn something about narrative.

Because even though he's never dominant unless I set it up, Gavin-the-Producer does play a very pedagogic role. The purpose of these emails, in fact, of all pornography, is to turn him on and get him off. And when I do this, Gavin rewards me promptly with a call. But I also want for him fall in love with me, i.e., find me the most adorable intriguing creature. Therefore, I experiment. How much is it possible to reveal without abandoning the point, the main event? Can seduction, i.e., a referencing of shared perceptions and experiences in the phenomenal and social world, augment the masturbatory objective of the text? Gavin's take on this is less complex. *I'm a storyteller*, he likes, like all the people in the film world like, to say. I never could relate to this, and I realize now, the problem with the movie *Gravity & Grace* was that it was less a story than a parable. It occurs to me, the emails that I'm writing him take place somewhere in between the genres of a psychological narrative and the picaresque. Perhaps pornography lends itself more easily to the rambling observations of the picaresque? It could be that the spaces in between the nexus-points of Fuck can be pure play. At any rate, when the email are done well, Gavin prints them out and compliments me by using them as an aid to jerking off. He doesn't like philosophy, finds it completely unerotic, an evasion of the point, which is always psycho-biological: His Rock Hard Cock My Limpid Cunt Our Pounding Hearts. History, humor and geography are easier to slip through –

Last night I opened Netscape, brought up the email I've been writing to him for the past six days and finally pushed "Send." I felt the message moving through the phone line in East Hampton westward to our servers in Los Angeles, then east again to a satellite above Nairobi: 15 seconds, a techno-logical eternity, the black horizontal bar expanding unretractably across the screen of the computer like a slow kiss or a fuck.

taputaro@ibm.net, 11/19/98 8:10 A.M., blanket

To: taputaro@ibm.net
From: ckraus@pacbell.net
Subject: blanket

Dear Africa,
    Well, now I'm lying on the cellar floor, blanketed, hands tied, but feeling very blissful, open, because I've just come two or three times while you were completely dominating me. Your voice was so specific, grounded & precise, it gave me something to hold onto as I moved outside my body. Until you took the plastic rod, hit my breasts and stomach, flipped the chair and whipped my ass & shoulders, I never quite believed that s/m was what you wanted. Thought you were just playing with the signs. My breathing's jagged, broken. Just two days ago I was writing in my diary how I agreed with the philoso-

pher Michel Foucault that sexuality is not the most intimate, identifying thing about a person. Thinking about acting, I said 'gesture' – but now I'm blown away and not so sure.

The blanket's scratchy and the cellar floor is hard.

Foolishly, I've been orbiting so fast inside the blanket that I stopped listening for your footsteps. And now the elevator arrives, opens, closes. Its mechanical hum fades out like the gong in Peter's Sagaponack zendo. Now I don't know where you are & can't see anything cause the blanket's covering my eyes.

And then there's just a lot of sadness – feeling so abandoned and exposed. It's like the world is flat & what lies around the edges of it is a hyperspace of dense emotion w/ sadness at its core. I know it's possible to leave & not come back & I don't know anything about you – don't know where or who you are.

Here are two things I've been able to surmise: 1) you have a relatively short attention span; 2) however, when your attention is engaged you are amazingly attentive and responsive. How will these two tendencies play out around the s/m safety question, Should the Dom ever really leave the sub alone?

Then I hear the elevator coming back. Doors open. When you pick me up inside the blanket, carrying me back into the elevator I know I'll never know.

Outside the eucalyptus leaves are shivering. I reach for you, hands pressed against your chest through the blanket, words tumbling out but you just say "Shhhh." You walk across the parking lot to your car, put the blanket(me) inside the trunk, slam the door and Off we go!...

In the next scene, we're sitting on the steps at Griffith Park. It's after midnight and you've given me some clothes. "You have to tell me now," you say, "if you want this to continue." I nod and even blush. "Right," you say, "then these will be the rules:

1. You will speak to me in words of just two syllables or less, and only when you have permission
2. You will come within five seconds of being told
3. You will not come or touch me without first asking my permission
4. I will punish you every time you break these rules..."

I agree to everything. Two hours later we're at an afterhours lounge bar east of Altadena. The people here are very old –

[Hi Africa here's the next installment. Is it cynical to try & turn someone on & entertain them? Surely no. I'm going to my house upstate for Thanksgiving, back on Sunday night. Hope things go well – x, chris]

Like I said, it took me six days to compose this, because when Gavin called last Friday, the scene we played was so compelling and disturbing that for one whole day I couldn't do anything at all. He called at three and when I looked outside the bedroom window it had already gotten dark. The broken oil tank propped up against the wall beside the window was mysteriously gone. The men from Hampton Gas must've been outside with blowtorches dismantling it. I didn't see or hear them. The phone was propped between my ear and shoulder underneath the feather comforter. I was following the sound of Gavin's voice as he moved around the basement. It was the first time Gavin topped me without any help at all, and when he came his breathing sounded like the wind moving through the brittle pampas-grass of Africa. *Well, how was that for phone sex?* Gavin asked, and then he said goodnight, the phone clicked off –

Sadness is the thing I'm moving towards. Some recognition of it as a philosophical position. "Simone Weil was the most radical philosopher of sadness," I've said or written every single time I've tried explaining *Gravity & Grace*, that wretched film. Plagued by headaches, vomiting, picking grapes and doing piecework in a factory, Simone Weil willed herself with all her strength into a place of weakness that was true to her "disturbing vision."

A single moment of true sadness connects you instantly to all the suffering in the world. In Mexico City last summer at the Chipultepec Avenue Zoo, surrounded by animals and children I was "seized by an unnameable emotion" and suddenly burst into tears. The idea that you are momentarily outside your body because *something else is speaking to you*.

It could be that sadness is the girl-equivalent to chance. Chance has always been equivalent to sadness, it is an interior reality so physical and large there is no need to access it by studying the mathematical laws of permutation. Do numbers exist outside the atmosphere, like stars? The 20th century male avant-garde, crocodiles in club chairs, studying chance as algebraic code... Chance is 'work' and 'work' is always something quantifiable. *Trace the line between two points*... Competing with her mathematician-brother since she was a tiny child, Simone Weil constantly regretted her deficiency in math and wished she had another lifetime she could spend in studying it. Like chance, emotion is a current that dissolves the boundaries of a person's subjectivity. It is a country. Shouldn't it be possible to leave the body? Is it wrong to even try?

The "she" in Fanny Howe's poetic novel *The Deep North* has trouble breathing, undergoes paroxysms of empathic fragmentation which she describes as panic attacks:

Nothing good flickered on the screen in her vision, but behind them was an emanation, a memory of emotion, of a time when the word and the thing were one and the same. To be saved by a word!...

But the first word was despair and it sailed into her vocabulary, like a tall ship from some haunted other time, tilting over a cold ocean. Despair, she realized, is what I'm feeling. It's an ancient feeling and is born in each person. Despair, the word, came like a sweet-dropping medicine, a coat of taste for her fear. Never had a word had such reverberating power for her. Never had one word been so strong it could humiliate all the little psychological bits and pieces, those labels that peeled off like slogans in the rain...

The desire to be worthy of some*thing*, some*one*.

The Statutory Regulations on Jews, issued by the Vichy government on October 3, 1940, prevented Jews from teaching in the public schools. Simone Weil received no answer to her request for a job teaching in the French university in Algeria and wrote an angry letter to the collaborationist French Minister of Education, seeking a precise definition of what it means to be a "Jew." This letter is cited often as evidence of Weil's self-loathing anti-Semitism. She was living with her parents in Marseilles who were waiting, like all the other Jews, for a visa, any visa, out of the country. Because she hated to waste time, she thought she'd use this limbo as a chance to pursue a dream she'd always had, of working as a farm-girl.

Most of Weil's new friends in Marseilles were Catholics. It was a religion she'd been flirting with since her disastrous experience in the Spanish Civil War. Simone Weil's history was a fairy tale, a joke. In August, 1936, she used her journalist's credentials to accompany a cadre of P.O.U.M. anarchists to the frontlines. Once there, she insisted on being issued with a rifle and allowed to join the fighting. She was clumsy and short-sighted. During target practice, everyone stayed clear of her. "Oh Lord," her comrades said, "deliver us from mousy women."

To her dismay, this war was nothing like the wars of ancient Greece. There were no prisoners. Anyone who was captured was immediately shot. Left back at camp with the cook while her cadre was blowing up a railway line, enemy aircraft circled overhead. She was very close to death and at that moment she looked up at the leaves and sky and everything seemed extraordinarily beautiful. The next day, short-sighted Simone stuck her leg into a pot of oil boiling on the campfire. Her parents caught the next train out of Paris and brought her safely home...

Still, in those two weeks of wartime she'd witnessed violence in its most essential state, where it becomes an end and not a means, a self-perpetuating panic. Back in Paris, she suffered terribly from headaches. And maybe it was her witnessing in Spain the ends of the ideology she'd so passionately embraced, or maybe it was the way the Spanish sky and trees had reached to her when she was certain she'd be shot, but the following year she spent the whole of Easter week in an abbey at Solesmes listening to Gregorian chants and found that listening was a way to ease her headaches. "Each sound," she reported later, "hit me like a blow; by an extreme effort of concentration I was able to rise above this wretched flesh, to leave it to suffer by itself, heaped up in a corner, and to find a pure and perfect joy in the unimaginable beauty of the of the chanting..."

In Paris, Weil copied out the words to a 17th century English poem called *Love* by George Herbert and as her stubborn hand was moving cross the page she felt an Alien spirit entering her body. From this time on, her thinking circled mostly around the possibility of love, God's love, as a redemptive end to suffering.

Stranded in Marseilles, Weil approached one of her Catholic acquaintances, Gustave Thibon, a priest and theologian who owned a farm near Avignon, and pleaded with him to let her be a laborer. In Avignon she perfected this technology of belief, translating the Lord's Prayer into Greek, lying in the fields and murmuring it. As she said the words, she entered hyperspace. Using the mystical-theatrical technique of repetition, her body was a telescope. Words lost, then found, their meaning. "For several days," she wrote, "I could not stop myself from saying it over and over all the time. At times the words tear my thoughts from my body and transport them to a place outside of space. Space opens up—"

Acting, my friend Lee Breuer says, is emotion transported through a culture.

IN NEW Zealand, Chev and I cut our vacation short, drove back to Auckland. On the way home, I stopped at a payphone and called up an Auckland artist, Evie Mason, I'd hung out with last time around, to say I was in town. To my great surprise, she already knew, and had organized a dinner. That night, ten of Evie's friends who were working film crew jobs came round. She'd already sent them copies of the script.

"This," she said, "will be your crew." All of them had read about American guerrilla filmmaking. It was a myth. It was a blue sky opportunity. While normally they were working as prop runners, focus pullers, second or third assistants on TV dramas and commercials, here they could be in charge of *whole departments* on a feature. They loved the project. The fact that there was no producer, or that I'd never made a normal film before, just didn't seem to figure.

The New Zealand Film Commission likes to boast to international producers in search of cheap, controllable locations, that the country offers film crews who are technically well-trained and efficient, and this was definitely true. Within four weeks, the core group of ten had multiplied itself to a 75-person call sheet. There were two production managers, 32 locations to arrange, insurance bonds, location permits. There were professional caterers, a six-person art department, cellphones, walkie-talkies, and a small fleet of leased production vehicles. A bunch of them had just come off the CIBY 2000 production of Jane Campion's *The Piano*, they must've still thought they were there. How was Helen Benneham's $40,000 ever going to pay for this?

Everyday from 8 'til 8, Delphine Bower and I sat in the Grey Lynn townhouse that was now the *Gravity & Grace* production office, working the phones. Coordinating actor's schedules, begging Volvo NZ to loan us a car, hustling cheap plane tickets, product placements, a dozen tulip plants to be grown especially for Scene 1, out of season. Helen Benneham flew up from Wellington and wished us well. The deal with her still held. So I didn't really worry all that much when the movie started going over budget. The US dollar was trading nearly double and we'd just raised $20,000 in New York to shoot Part 2. If Sylvère and I could could just hold on and see it through, we'd save it back when Helen kicked in her promised second $40,000...

The demands of the production multiplied and every day we struggled to keep up with it. We were running towards a finish line that kept receding. Sometimes Delphine's young friends dropped by and this was comforting. None of them had jobs. They woke up at 10 and spent the daylight hours sitting around and drinking cups of tea, reading newspapers and smoking. I liked it that the front room of the production office felt like the dayroom in a nursing home. Except the phones kept ringing –

Four weeks before production started, we lost the Director of Photography, Dennis Miller, an experienced DP who everyone had said would *make* the movie. Dennis got a better job. There was no one else around. Frantic, I hired Colleen Sweeney, who loved the script but had only ever focus-pulled because of the rampant sex discrimination in the New Zealand film industry.

Colleen asked to see the storyboards. I panicked. I couldn't draw and had no visual sense at all. The idea that scenes in movies were composed of shots of varying durations was mysterious and murky. Should we see the characters straight-on, or at an angle? I didn't know. Why here and why not there? How do poets know where to break a line of poetry? The idea of "movie" was a mesh of words and voices and emotion which I'd just assumed that Dennis would know how to translate. I'd never thought of movies visually before; could hardly tell the difference between a two-shot and a closeup.

And so by February, although I'd only been in Auckland

for six weeks, it seemed I'd left Sylvère and Lily back in Easton for a decade. And then Sylvère called up one night and said I have bad news –

It is so difficult now to find the proper tone or pitch to write about the death of our dog Lily. It is November 24. Tomorrow afternoon I'm leaving for six days to go upstate for Thanksgiving. In the car back from the beach today I fantasized a heartrending tour-de-force, Flaubert meets *Little Dorritt*, but now it just seems silly.

For weeks Sylvère's devoted calls and faxes hid the fact that Lily was getting sicker, but finally late in February, he explained. Lily's tumor was untreatable. Even though she couldn't speak , he could see she was in enormous pain. Her lungs were filling up with phlegm, she had difficulty breathing. Visits to the vet on College Hill became routine. They pumped her lungs and gave her canine morphine. One afternoon the vet suggested it might be time to end her suffering, but it was too abrupt, he wasn't ready. Sylvère asked the vet to pump her lungs out one more time so they could have one final night together. And as I'm writing this, I'm crying – the image of Sylvère, then 56 years old, alone in the rented house in Easton, cradling the dying dachshund. "She looked at me," he said. "She understood…"

The image catapults me still into a grief that's bottom-less because it's absolute, unspoken. What I loved most about Sylvère was his capacity for sentiment. We had no children. With Lily gone, was there really any need for us to stay together? She was the thing that passed between us beyond words, our talisman, our victim. She was a medium of pure comprehension.

Alone in Auckland with Delphine the phones kept

ringing and I could not stop crying. Crying leads you through concentric rings of sadness. You close your eyes and travel outwards through a vortex that draws you towards the saddest thing of all. And the saddest thing of all isn't anything but sadness. It's too big to see or name. Approaching it's like seeing God. It makes you crazy. Because as you fall you start to feel yourself approaching someplace from which it will not be possible to retrace your steps back out – it's much too large and ancient. There are too many parts of other people in it for one person to absorb. Grief is *information*.

Sometime during the second night of non-stop crying my father called and said *You'd better stop*, and so I did, because I'd been crazy once already in New Zealand and I remembered, crazy women hardly get to speak, let alone make movies.

Sylvère sent one of our most beautiful photographs of Lily – looking straight at us, her floppy ears spread out as she treads water in a lilypond, as innocent as Millais' *Ophelia*. Two weeks later for my birthday, Colleen gave me a little snapshot frame of precious woods to keep it in and I was deeply touched. So when the deal she said she'd wrangled with the lighting rental house fell through and the bill came due $3,000 over budget, there was nothing else to do but pay it.

For this, her first dramatic feature, Colleen's equipment rental list included two truckloads full of giant lights called HMIs, dolly tracks and cart, a mini-crane. It took five people to operate all this: two licensed grips, three gaffers. Colleen and I decided that the movie should look lyrical. Together, we planned an establishing shot of a luxury hotel by night that had nothing much to do with the dramatic action of the movie. To light it, Colleen hired a special light mounted on a flatbed truck, operated by a special hired man, that was powerful enough to illuminate an entire city block. I wrote another check. It was too late to change it. The movie was completely uncontrollable. Each department had become a kingdom of its own, dedicated to the career advancement of its members and I knew nothing about any of it. They were labor, I was management. As the first day of production loomed, the First AD tried patiently to instruct me in the rudiments of filmmaking. My eyes glazed over. There was something about the "left-right rule" and some other thing about how the camera couldn't "cross the line" because it screwed up continuity. But still, there is a logic to this movie, I kept thinking, and it lives in me –

"Why," Sylvère asks me to this day, "would anyone with so little visual imagination as you ever want to be a filmmaker?"

Outside the oak trees here in Northwest Woods are a brittle rusty monochrome. Gavin Brice's movie in North Africa wraps in two more weeks. I'm only here another month. It's the last day of November. There is this idea I've always had, of "movie." Last weekend in the southern Adirondacks my friend Warren arrived late Wednesday afternoon, the day before Thanksgiving. The house was full so I drove him over to the Northwoods Club, the place that Howard Cook took over when they sold the store. Howard rents out rooms but the place is empty, no one wants it.

We stopped by the bar to get the keys from Howard. It was one of those gray late afternoons when clouds hang halfway down the hills and night seeps in before the day has even started, and as we ran up the hill I flashed back to the first time I'd ever made a movie. Warren had been there too.

There'd been a dozen people who didn't really know each other, traveling in a van from New York City, to act out fragments of *King Lear* in an abandoned building. Same trees, same weather, different hills. The moment when we all stepped outside the van was deeply thrilling. Annie started filming, Jeff took stills. Twelve strangers walking down the road with coats and bags, stopping, starting. It was an epistomological joke, a metaphor for the interrupted mental flow when memory becomes nostalgia. There was no script, no shot list, but the movie had a logic.

"The director's job is quality control," they said before we started shooting *Gravity & Grace*. And I could not relate. I thought the director's job was more like being a dinner party hostess or an electrical transformer. You're driving north and a Jimmie Rodgers song comes on the radio just as the mountains come in view. Great happiness! The idea of movie is that each person enters as a character. Their faces on the screen contain their entire histories *to that point* but through the very act of entering the movie, these histories change, combine. The idea of movie is *a powerful explosive will towards happiness* (as Walter Benjamin said of Proust): emotional logic attained through a poetics of didacticism.

A third production manger, Judy Sargent, joined the *Gravity & Grace* crew about two weeks before the movie started. Judy, 25, was just finishing a TV stint on *Playschool*. The other two production managers claimed we couldn't shoot the film without her. Together, they formed a Politbureau. They summoned me to a meeting in a freezing loft to talk about personnel relations. There'd been complaints, they said, about Delphine. My relationship with her was privileged. There was no longer room in the production hierarchy, they said, for Delphine to be my personal assistant. I was Lear, stripped of a retinue of one. I protested. They saw this coming. If I insisted that Delphine remain, she'd have to have a real job with a title; say, for instance, Second Assistant Wardrobe Runner? Because most of us were girls, it was suggested that this well-boundaried demotion would be better for Delphine Bower's self-esteem. I swallowed hard. And, oh yes, we were another several thousand dollars over budget now? Luckily Sylvère was visiting.

Seventy three people showed up at Alicia Stone's house (the primary location) on the first day of the shoot at 5 a.m. The caterers set up a tent. There was a special guy to make the coffee. There were wardrobe vans and trailers, a diesel generator, two makeup girls, the grips and gaffers, prop stand-by, art department, several runners. The lead electrician, Colleen's friend, had flown up (at our expense) six hundred miles from Invercargill. Everyone agreed we should be shooting at a ratio of 7:1. That is, for every take we used, six takes would be discarded. In Scene One, Ceal unfurls a bedsheet and lays it on the bed. This simple action took three hours.

Everyone was working very hard to art direct and shoot and light and sound record some footage that would be an asset to their reels. The movie was a calling card for hustling work on the bigger movies that they hoped to work on. The actors, who I loved, were an inconvenience to be tolerated. There was my friend, the poet Alan Brunton, who'd become a distinguished person since the last time that I saw him, studying vaudeville in an old Times Square hotel. There was Therese O'Connell, who'd led the feminist takeover of the Wellington Youth Anarchist Society fifteen years ago and gone on to found an immigrant resettlement center. Everything about Therese was huge: her warmth and leadership and humor. There was the actress Jennifer Ludlam, who'd just won Best Supporting Actress. She was playing Ceal against her agent's better judgment, and every move she made was colored by intelligence, compassion. To my mind these people were like National Living Treasures, though to the crew they were no more important than the dolly tracks or rented conifers.

By noon we'd been on the set for seven hours. We still hadn't filmed scene two, and there were another 165 scenes to go. Seventy-three people hovered waiting to perform their mostly fabricated jobs. Every set-up lasted several hours. The camera rehearsals took so long that makeup had to swoop back in before we started shooting. Was makeup even necessary in a wideshot? It didn't matter. By day three, *Playschool* Judy told me that we'd have to drop some scenes. And even then, there was no time to rehearse the most dramatically important scenes. What really was important? It was *important* to place and light two potted pine-trees; it was *important* to rehearse a bumpy tracking shot a dozen times even though the shot just moved from A to B and had no words and no performance.

By the middle of week one, most of the conversation on the set revolved around boasts about how little everybody slept. Four hours? Three? Sleep deprivation was an emblem of professionalism, and *things came out*, although they weren't supposed to. Production halted for three hours when Delphine eloped in tears with one of the rented art department vans. The head of wardrobe had just screamed at her, something about forgetting Ceal's white shoes that matched her car. When Delphine and the shoes were finally recovered, we pulled the shot. The frameline ended just above her ankles. Ceal's feet were never even in the scene.

THE HOUSE I'm living in on Seacrest Lane is cold and drafty. I spend a lot of time in bed, dreaming, reading, drinking coffee. In the blanket email, I told Gavin I'd be back on Sunday, now it's Thursday. In the dream I had this morning, Sylvère and I went shopping for a jacket. It was a little plaid thing with toggles, for a boy. In the dream I'm feeling very "womanly" in a 1950s movie sense, as we're walking up Fifth Avenue, and Sylvère seems very "manly." I think that older women are technicians of the state, permitted to use language, concepts, literally, for their own sake, in exchange for keeping social order. Around 9 there was the most beautiful blinkered kind of light behind the trees. Gavin says he likes s/m because it returns us to a primal sense of what it means to be a man or woman.

The "idea of movie" is that emotion is a place. It's site-specific. Just as the optic nerve makes cubist cut-ups out of objects for the brain to reassemble, emotion happens in and out. It is a symbiotic loop, a country that we enter through our bodies.

"Considerate people clean up after their pets," the sign at Main Beach in East Hampton advises. The public signage here, just like the landscape, is so genteel. Everything is muffled in a kind of cotton batting. At dusk, when the docents close the split-rail gate and drive home for supper in their Volvos, the Mashomack Preserve becomes an enchanted kingdom of wild animals. There are topiary hedges, rolling lawns, beach-grass full of butterflies, October's sharp protuberance of Montauk daisies. The cottages have porch gazebos, cupolas and tiny shingled eyebrow windows. Dreams of caramel-colored Shetland ponies replace dreams of sadomasochism.

VERY LITTLE has been written within philosophy that treats emotion as an active state of consciousness. Writing in 1948 in *The Emotions Outline of a Theory*, Jean-Paul Sartre rejects this possibility. "We are afraid," he writes, "because we flee." He says emotion is escape, escape from what? A flight into a magical world that offers refuge from the need to act "responsibly." Emotion has no reality or integrity. It's a default; an imaginary world constructed by a frightened individual.

Warren Neidich, an artist and neurobiological theorist whose work revolves around a questioning of optical perception, believes that certain drugs engender a parallel set of memories. For several months one time he smoked a lot of pot, and was amazed to find that being stoned transported him to a consciousness that had a separate continuity. Getting high, he picked up threads of memories and conversations begun the last time he was high that he forgot as soon as he came down. THC, he says, sets off an entirely separate memory system. There is a neural network, ordinarily dormant within the body, that is sensitive to THC. "Turning on" means literally turning on a secondary neural network through which experience is received throughout the body.

Therefore, if "identity" is really just a process of association, Warren Neidich and Warren Neidich Stoned are two entirely different people.

Marijuana, according to Neidich's observation, is then a biological equivalent to the Aboriginal sense of history – a parallel universe in which the living are connected to the past by dreaming dreams of their dead ancestors. I ask Warren if emotion is like THC. He doesn't answer. Does sadness, panic, grief, unlock a roadmap that takes us further out into the heart of sadness?

Sartre develops his theory of emotion-as-denial by citing case studies of female neurasthenics under the treatment of psychiatrist Pierre Janet. These girls broke down in tears when granted audiences with the doctor. Charged with rationally explaining their unhappiness, they found that they could not. And so they cried. Janet explains these outbursts of emotion as a setback. Sartre seeks a more behavioral analysis. The girl who cries instead of talks is not merely defaulting to what Sartre calls "inferior" behavior... the girl is after all, a girl. She is attempting to manipulate her doctor.

"A sick girl comes to Janet; she wants to confide the secret of her inner turmoil. But she is unable to; such social behavior is too hard for her. *Then* she sobs. But does she sob *because* she cannot say anything? Or does she sob precisely *in order to not say anything?*... There she was in a narrow and threatening world which expected her to perform a precise act... Janet himself indicated by his attitude that he was listening and waiting. But at the same time, his presence, his personality, repelled this confession. It was necessary to escape this intolerable tension by... turning her attention back to herself, by transforming Janet from a judge to a comforter... Lacking the will and power to accomplish the acts she had been planning, the girl behaves in such a way that the universe no longer requires anything of her... She wanted to replace Janet's attitude of impassive waiting to one of affectionate concern. That is what she wanted." (Sartre, *The Emotions Outline of a Theory*)

I think emotion is like hyperspace, a second set of neural networks becoming active in the body. I think "the girl" was right. Sartre thinks that those who experience an intolerable situation through their bodies are manipulative cowards. It's inconceivable to him that female pain can be impersonal. And so, like all the female anorexics and the mystics, "the girl" can only be a brat. She is *starving* for attention.

WHEN ALDOUS Huxley took mescalin in Los Angeles in 1954 he experienced an expanded sense of simultaneity. *Each person is at each moment capable of remembering all that has ever happened to him and of perceiving everything that is happening everywhere in the universe.* The brain's eliminative, not productive. Mescalin, like speed, contains a chemical that stimulates production of adrenaline. And this is really interesting, because Huxley's recognition of an information-flood runs parallel to the Gnostic sense that we are living in a continuous present which was described by sci-fi writer Philip K. Dick *under the influence of amphetamine.* In *Valis,* Dick discovers that the Gnostic empire never ended. The universe operates according to the laws of phylogenic memory; i.e., each person carries in their body an entire memory of the species. Gnostic beliefs are founded on a technology of resurrection. At death, the spirit engrams itself into a code that travels back into the world as *information*. "The universe," Dick writes, "is information, and we are static in it. The information fed to us we hypostatize into the phenomenal world..." The Gnostics live forever via techno-transmigration symbiotically absorbed among the living. Therefore, each person is capable not just of perceiving everything at once, but of *becoming other people*.

Warren called back and says he thinks emotion maybe is produced as biologic memory. I ask him to explain. He says that certain situations trigger memories of others. There is a genealogical memory-network within the body's neurons, looping round itself like closed-circuit TV. But what makes it possible, then, to remember things that haven't actually happened to us at all? To experience a radical form of empathy and be seized, like Simone Weil, by a sadness so enormous it creates a panic for *the good*? In Warren's view, sadness is a cottage industry. I think emotion's like the global flow of capital.

GAVIN BRICE still hasn't called since I emailed him two weeks ago, lying wrapped up in a blanket on the cellar floor, and I'm wondering if it's 'cause he didn't like the part I wrote to him about sadness. *It's like the world is flat and all around the edges of it there is a hyperspace of emotion with sadness at its core...* Imaginary sex with him has become a way to mark the absent LA landscape. There are certain corresponding numbers in the telephonic pit. He calls and gets me on the line. I'm hooked, I answer. The telephone is an instrument of telepathy. It doesn't matter what we do, it's where and how we do it. The bar in Chinatown at Hop Louie, the Whitley Terrace condo, the parking lot behind the Dresden turn into landmarks where it is *absence* that excites. In this way, LA becomes a neural roadmap.

Last night I dreamt that Gavin Brice's name was Roger Gavin and he was visiting me in a rented flat on Aro Street I shared in Wellington with my sister, Carol. It turned out that Roger/Gavin hadn't really been in Africa, nor was he a studio film producer. He was 27, tall and shaggy. He'd just been "overseas" and Roger/Gavin bragged to us about the cheap hotel he'd found in Paris. I kept wondering when we'd fuck, and kept sending covert-roommate messages to my sister, but she stayed right there in the kitchen chopping vegetables.

In scene two, Roger/Gavin's in my bedroom near the porch. We're on the bed. The sex we had was like New Zealand sex, experimental touch, a hazy kind of groping between two mammals. There was hardly any kind of female/male polarity, or if there was, we found it accidentally. It was interspecies sex between a bear and a raccoon and in the dream I remember that I liked this –

"Roger" was my friend Penny's boyfriend's name in Wellington. Like Chev, he was one of the few real 'workers' in the Revolutionary Workers' Party. He was an authentic prole: a union leader at the meatworks. He drank and beat his girlfriend up and unlike Chev, he had no capacity for sentiment –

Aldous Huxley didn't trip alone. He had a psychedelic guide. The hills were getting shaded in Coastal Canyon in the late afternoon when he was coming down. He'd been studying Cezanne's *Self-Portrait* when the guide instructed him to shut his eyes and look inside. He found the inscape "curiously unrewarding." Earlier that afternoon he'd been entering the Red Hot Poker blossoms in his garden and realized they were "passionately alive, standing on the very brink of utterance." He looked down at the leaves and discovered "a cavernous intricacy of the most delicate green lights and shadows, pulsing." But when he closed his eyes, the guide asked him what he saw inside and he complained that it was cheap and trivial. Like Simone Weil, Huxley was impatient with the boundaries of him-"self" and longed to attain a state of decreation. "This suffocating interior of a dimestore ship," he says, "was my own personal self." He discovers that he loathes this culture because it "attaches more importance to the inscape than to objective referents… that retreats into an investigation of the personal as opposed to the more than personal." Mescalin has an important purpose in the future: it is "a chemical vacation from intolerable selfhood."

Huxley is not a manipulative girl. He is a distinguished and credentialed thinker, and so we take him at his word. Yet why do Weil's interpreters look for hidden clues when she argues, similarly, for a state of decreation? She hates herself, she can't get fucked, she's ugly. If she finds it difficult to eat, it must be that she's refusing food, as anorexics do, as an oblique manipulation. "The girl" in Sartre and Janet's narrative breaks down in order to gain sympathy and draw attention. Anything a female person says or does is open to "interpretation." If the female anorexic isn't consciously manipulative, then she's tragic: shedding pounds in a futile effort to erase her female body, which is the only part of her that's irreducible and defining.

It's the beginning of December and it's cold. A month ago I was biking to the East Hampton Free Public Library and copying down the names of flowers from a 1920s illustrated handbook: purple milkwort, evening primrose, queen anne's lace, spotted cowbane, sparkleberry, smooth azalea... It bothers me that Gavin hasn't called, and so this morning, underneath the featherbed, I dreamed him. I was in the hospital on IV. Sylvère was there, and my friend Jim Fletcher, and then Gavin called and I realized in the dream that I was dreaming it to make myself feel better. I got up and wrote another email –

Dear Africa,

Strange not to've heard from you for so long. I guess there's no etiquette for phone sex, but I'm wondering if you're busy or you disliked my last email or you're just not inclined to do this anymore. Please don't just drop out of sight – x chris

Tonight I sent it. Right now it's very difficult to eat.

It could be, people dream to close the gaps between conscious thought and memory.

5.

DREAMS

Q: What is the difference between the "sign" and the "symbol"?

A:

IN THE dream last night of New York City a person was noticing a jar of purple roses on someone's table. One of the roses moved from the glass jar on the table into the person's dream that night. This movement was a kind of object-transmigration. It spanned several feet and 28 hours. (In the dream, time and space are separate entities and don't exist simultaneously.) And then the rose begins appearing in other people's dreams, randomly and multipally. All these people walking through the signage-saturated streets of New York City, the imprint of the purple rose pulsing through them like a chemical tattoo. The rose becomes an icon, a heraldic symbol.

(As I write these lines, I stop to check the actual meaning of the word 'transmigration'. There is a Webster's *New Collegiate Dictionary* on the bookshelf underneath the penis shrine, and *it comes as no surprise* to find that fifteen purple rose petals are pressed between the pages that I open to…)

Gavin calls five minutes after I find the purple rose petals. *Hi*, he says, *It's Africa.* That also comes as no surprise.

"WHAT IS the reason that as soon as one human being shows he needs another(no matter whether his need be slight or great) the latter draws back from him? Gravity." (Simone

Weil, *Gravity and Grace*)

All her life, Simone Weil was acutely conscious of the collapse of beauty. As a child, she loved fairy tales and nature walks. She hated dolls. She made up games based on her favorite stories of the Greeks and Romans. She had an older brother, Andre, who she copied and adored. They were a conspiracy of two. Sometimes on the bus, to the horror of their mother, they hid their socks and shoes and pretended they were neglected children. She was a roving ball of curiosity who never slowed down long enough to see herself as a pretty child, which was of course how others saw her. The child-Simone had an exaggerated sense of fairness. She thought if everybody dressed alike, there would be no more war between the classes. Some people experience a rupture with their identity as children. Others remain faithful to it all their lives. All her life, Simone Weil sought increasingly complex articulations of her visions as a child. They were never fundamentally revised. The child-Simone experienced the world as a rush of passionate sensations. The philosopher-Simone, after studying epistemology, came to call these sensations *knowledge*.

At 14, she crashed headlong up against her limitations and this recognition caused her great despair. Her brother Andre was a mathematical prodigy. He was lost to her and so she felt like she'd lost everything. She was not a genius, not a pretty girl. She couldn't sing or dance or paint; she had no talents. Simone realized, in her adolescent clarity, that the only card she had to play was her intelligence. It didn't seem like very much. And yet, she realized, when she decided not to kill herself, if she worked day and night and focused all her will and longing on a single object, it might still be possible to do *something* worthwhile… And this, she knew, was true for anyone at all. Weil's awareness of her personal imperfections made her sensitive to all the imperfections in the world. She didn't really see the differences between them. A life well spent meant vanquishing these imperfections: to try, by focusing all one's energy and attention, *to make things right*.

Fairy tales are parables. They are yearnings towards *the good* in an imperfect world. The first story Weil remembered was a fairy tale her mother told when she was four. *Marie in Gold, Marie in Tar.* Good Marie is banished by her stepmother to the forest. She approaches a house that has two doors. A woman asks her to come in, but first Marie must choose a door: the door in tar, the door in gold. Good Marie sees very little difference between gold and tar. She chooses tar, and as she walks across the portal, gold coins pour down around her. She takes them home. Stepmother sees a chance to score. She sends her daughter, Bad Marie, back to the woods to get more gold but when Bad Marie crosses what she thinks will be the golden door, the tar rains down.

The headaches started when Weil was studying for her exams at the Ecole Normale. They lasted all her life. She never knew when they would start, or why, or how long they would last for. When the headaches hit, the rest of her went limp. *Feeling your head exploding. Feeling your brain on the point of bursting to bits. Feeling your spine jammed up into your brain and feeling your brain like a dried fruit…* The headaches made her nauseous, dizzy. She couldn't eat or drink; even chewing made her vomit. She felt as if her head was being pressed inside a vice.

Years later she was writing in her notebook about beauty. She listed three criteria. Beauty is a harmony of chance and of *the good*. It's irreducible and seems as if it's been there always, and yet it is obedient to a higher law, a force of love and altruism that Weil's thought always returns to, which she calls *the good*. Beauty, like God, is both intensely personal and impersonal. In the face of it, there is no more desire. "We want to *eat* all the other objects of desire. The beautiful is that which we desire without wishing to eat it. We desire that it should be…"

To tell a story is an act of love. The teller reaches deep inside the listener's mind and offers rest and order where there would otherwise be none. The fairy tale does not deny the chaos of the universe. Rather, it offers the chance, the possibility, that in a less than perfect world, it might still be possible to *do something* that's good.

When she was 15, her wealthy cultured parents took her to a spa. While her mother took the cure, she smoked and gossiped with the chambermaids and porters and urged them all to unionize. The rhetoric of Marxism appealed to her, but still, she told her girlfriend Simone Petrement, she found the workers much more *beautiful* than the clients at the spa. She wrote letters seeking to join the Communist Party, and later on she did.

When she was 22 and teaching high school in Le Puy, she spent her days off traveling to a mining town, St. Etienne, to teach free classes in French language and political economy. "In Marx's eyes, perhaps the most important conquest of the proletarian revolution should be the abolition of what he calls 'the degrading division of work into intellectual and manual work.' …To this end, we must, first of all, give the workers the ability to handle language and especially the written language," she wrote in the leftist magazine,

L'Effort.

In Le Puy, she successfully led the Teachers' Union to form an inter-union movement with the bricklayers and carpenters. The fact that there was no union for the unemployed appalled her, and she undertook to unionize them also. She led a hundred of them to a meeting of the City Council. When they were denied the right to speak, they marched in front of the Council table before proceeding to the mayor's house. These events were described locally as a "riot."

She was reprimanded by the school administration not only for her politics, but for behavior inappropriate to a girl's philosophy professor. She'd been seen in town sharing drinks and talks and handshakes with the filthy unemployed. "I refuse," she said, "to answer any questions about my personal life."

She didn't heat or clean her house. It was a happy time. She lived on cocoa and potatoes and adrenaline.

Weil complained in her union newspaper that the administration "still regards certain people as untouchables." The unemployed were given work, and the National Teacher's Union leadership defended her. She wrote more articles, she taught, she spoke at meetings.

Still, years later, it was the distance she perceived between the union leadership and the workers who they claimed to represent that led her to abandon French left-electoral politics. Weil was driven by a panic of altruism, an empathy so absolute she couldn't separate the suffering that she witnessed from her own. She wanted politics to be a fairy tale, an attempt against all odds to make things right. Sometimes when the headaches hit, she looked inside. Pain marked the meeting place between her soul and body, the center of the nervous system. Always, she was terrified that she might waste her life.

THE FIRST or second time I talked with Gavin, he told me how he once believed in politics. *We used to think*, he said, *that we could change the world.* He laughed. *Although now we know much better.* This morning on the phone we had a fight. Three weeks ago he'd left me shuddering in a blanket in the cellar of a Whitley Terrace condo, and I'd been blown away, and then he hadn't called, and even though we talked a dozen times I didn't know if I would ever hear from him again. Because maybe things, i.e., the sex we had, had gotten to a certain point he thought he wanted and once they did, he might as well cut out. Was I totally expendable? Did the fact that phone sex is anonymous mean the normal rules of considerate behavior don't apply?

But wait, he said. *You're not anonymous.* I heard him smile. But I was shaking. *We have to make a deal*, I said. *If you want to keep on doing this, you can't just disconnect. You can stop any time you want, but first you have to tell me.* But what I didn't know was that the mainframe server in Nairobi had been down for several days, and then they'd been away a week, shooting in the jungle, but still he understood. *I can't promise that I'll contact you according to your wants or expectations, but I promise you I'll never disconnect –*

And then he asked if I would tell him another story. It was a fairy tale about being bound and whipped and gagged by someone who did not attract or interest me at all, in

Irvine, California. The story had an s/m moral: it isn't chemistry or personality that counts, *it's what you do*. This is a quantum leap beyond modernism's ethos of transgression, in which eroticism arises from disgust. Disgust implies duality; requires content. But now that there's no longer any meaning in the landscape, it is possible to fabricate desire anywhere. The technology of s/m transforms neutrality into content.

But Gavin was much more interested in the part about the margarita in the dog dish. And so I told him all about the butt plugs and the nipple clamps. I gave him bits of dialogue – *Oh my you have a nice big hairy twat* – and in between the climaxes I turned the story back on him and asked him questions. He told me that he cared for me and that I'd *very subtly, very nicely*, managed all our conversations, which was what producing means to him, and then he thanked me. The story was a reconciliation.

WHEN SHE was 24, Simone Weil published a controversial article in a magazine called *Proletarian Revolution* challenging the left's conventional wisdom about fascism. At that time, in the early 30s, fascism was a threat not taken seriously. It was seen as "capitalism's last card." But Weil had visited Germany and saw the beginning of a technocratic state that was not dissimilar from Stalin's. The bureaucratic states of Germany and Russia weren't aberrations from the proletarian movement. They were its vanguard. And yet the article, called *Prospects*, was not a recantation of left politics. Rather, she asked her readers to embrace the hopelessness of their cause while moving forward.

In the last two weeks while hoping Gavin Brice would call, I've been studying his favorite writer, Joseph Conrad. Both Weil and Conrad share a narcissistic heroism. Although, perhaps since Conrad's male, his self-love is channeled through a quest for personal identity. He wants to like the image of himself that is projected to the world, just as Weil would later on discover that to disappear is the quickest route to being truly admirable. In *The Secret Sharer*, Conrad writes: "I wondered how far I should turn out faithful to that ideal conception of one's own personality every man sets up for himself secretly." And in *The Heart of Darkness*: "I don't like work – no man does – but I like what is in the work, – the chance to find yourself. Your own reality –"

Weil was more ambitious. When she was 26 she took a leave from teaching philosophy to *lycèe* girls to become a factory worker. Weil took a piecework job on an assembly line producing cars. She wanted to know what workers know. She could barely make the quota. She wrote to a former student: "I am still unable to achieve the required speeds, for many reasons: my unfamiliarity with the work, my awkwardness, which is considerable, a certain natural slowness of movement, and a habit of thinking, which I can't shake off." And later, in her diary: *The feeling of personal dignity as it has been formed by society is shattered. One must forge another...* The factory year was Weil's first experience in decreation. Weil proved capable of using work as fervently to disappear as Conrad used it to become his ideal "I." And later: *If the 'I' is the only thing we truly own, we must destroy it –*

In *The Second Sex*, Weil's contemporary Simone de Beauvoir defines the origins of female narcissism through penis envy. The penis is an alter ego in which boys see themselves. This frees them to assume an attitude of subjectivity. But the girl cannot incarnate herself in any part of herself, and so she plays with dolls. *While the boy seeks himself in the penis as an autonomous subject, the little girl coddles her doll and dresses her as she dreams of being coddled and dressed up herself; she thinks of herself as a marvelous doll.*

At 18, Weil and de Beauvoir were classmates, competing to enter the prestigious Ecole Normale. (Weil came in first; de Beauvoir second.) Weil hoped to change the world. De Beauvoir hoped for an independence, an apartment, and that she'd have the chance to work instead of merely marrying. At school, Weil's nicknames were "the Red Virgin" and "the categorical imperative in skirts." Best known for her intelligence and her bizarre outfits, she dressed like a truck-driver, smoked hand-rolled cigarettes, and walked around with communist papers bulging from her pockets. For weeks, de Beauvoir watched Bizarre-Simone when they hung around the courtyard. She'd heard a story that Bizarre-Simone had wept when she'd read the news that a famine had broken out in China. *These tears*, de Beauvoir wrote much later, *compelled my respect much more than her gifts as a philosopher. I envied her for having a heart that beat around the world.*

Eventually, the two most brilliant girls of that Paris generation met. They sat around a cafe or a courtyard, debating what the point was. Bizarre-Simone declared in no uncertain terms that only one thing mattered: a revolution which would feed the starving people of the earth. Simone-the-Existentialist countered: "The problem's not to make men happy, but to find the reason for their existence." "It's easy to see," Bizarre-Simone snapped back, "you've never starved." They never spoke again. End of story, end of conversation.

When Weil's mystical writings were published posthumously in the volume *Waiting for God*, the critic Claude Mauriac discerned a certain "mutilation of heart" in Weil's will-to-decreation. A mutilation which, the critic argued, must have arisen from her ugliness, which is, he says, *the greatest unhappiness in a woman*. Is it any wonder that the two Simone's fought? Ugliness, unhappiness, emotion, female narcissism and manipulation –

EACH PERSON is at each moment capable of remembering all that has ever happened to him and of perceiving everything that is happening everywhere in the universe. Taking mescalin one afternoon in 1953, Aldous Huxley opens a book of Botticelli prints and trips out on the purple silk of pleated bodices, long wind-blown skirts and drapery. He looks at his legs and sees within the fabric of his pants a *labyrinth of endlessly significant complexity*. Mescalin and other psychedelic drugs allow visual information to penetrate the body's neural-optic screens. And yet we also, similarly, screen out moral information, perceiving wealth as if it existed by itself, as if wealth was not one side of a lopsided equation, supported on the other side by poverty.

A table is a mystical thing, Karl Marx wrote in Volume 1 of *Capital*. I wonder how he stood it. *Because in it the social character of men's labor appears to them as an objective character stamped upon the production of that labor...* He was talking about the fact that every object in the world is a summation of itself, of every one and every thing that made it, of how it came to be. It was analysis, and therefore separate from his *feelings*.

At 28, Marx wrote a poem called *Feelings*:

> *Heaven I would comprehend*
> *I would draw the world to me*
> *Loving, hating, I intend*
> *That my star shine brilliantly*

At 28, Weil was studying redemption. Her body was so saturated with content she felt her head would split apart. Listening to the chanting in an abbey: *Each sound hurt me like a blow; by an extreme effort of concentration I was able to rise above this wretched flesh, to leave it heaped up in a corner, and find a pure and perfect joy in the beauty of the chanting and the words… This experience made it possible for me to understand the possibility of divine love…*

And yet we admire and appreciate wealth's symbols without acknowledging wealth's abstracted sadism – WHAT, and at WHAT COST?

Aldous Huxley spent eight hours tripping out on mescalin

Simone Weil spent twenty years tripping out on content and causality

ALIENS & ANOREXIA

Is it any wonder that she starved?

Impossible to drink the coffee without thinking about the *finca* laborers who picked it, transported from their villages in cattle trucks to work for fifty cents a day… *Impossible* to view the paintings at the Frick Museum without thinking about the murdered workers, gunned down outside while protesting child labor… *Impossible* to admire a $2500 pair of shredded Perry Ellis jeans without thinking about the new South African government's decision to spend its limited AIDS budget on education rather than provide its 1 in 5 infected citizens with AZT…84 percent of the world's wealth is owned by 7 percent of its people, what exactly does this mean?… The shingled cottages out here on Further Lane are preserved by tearing up miles of desert outside of Albuquerque, New Mexico and filling it with strip malls …Investment: the most disembodied form of violence …*Impossible* to sit zazen in the 18th century stable exquisitely converted to a zendo here on Sagaponack Road without wondering who spawned the yields maintaining this estate …My first experience with sadism was in the Park Avenue penthouse of a bank executive, admiring the Haitian art up on the walls. I stammered, *It's a very violent country. Why yes,* he smiled… The true sophisticate has attained the psychological refinement to be aware not only of the work but of the cruelty that's fetishized in things – *Don't judge,* he says, *enjoy it.* Museum-quality tapestries from Port-au-Prince, hearts dripping sequined blood above the wing chairs – everything is tainted – **WHO MAKES YOUR LIFE POSSIBLE?** I want to scream.

The panic of altruism: sadness rests inside the body, always, nascent like the inflammation of a chronic disease.

Therefore, empathy is not a reaching outward. It is a loop. Because there isn't any separation any more between what you are and what you see.

> *A squirrel turning in its cage in a rotation of*
> *the celestial sphere. Extreme misery and extreme*
> *grandeur. It is when man sees himself as a*
> *squirrel turning round and round in a circular*
> *cage, that if he does not lie to himself, he is*
> *closest to salvation.*
>> – Simone Weil, *Gravity and Grace*

As a child, Weil found an expression of her longing for *the good* through fairy tales. Later, like all middle-class French teenagers, she read Greek philosophy at school. She loved Plato and Pythagoras for their sense of order. The proportion of Pythagoras' golden mean implied a search for equilibrium... a balance, human-scale, which like the moral of a fairy tale, is an arrival at *the good*, the only worthwhile destination. As a professional philosopher, Weil never left the Greeks behind. Rather, she sought out other articulations of this longing towards the good in other cultures. Greek thought became her golden mean for interpreting all the questions of her time. Weil assimilated her shock at mindless violence in the Spanish Civil War through a reading of *The Iliad*. Likewise, in *The Need for Roots*, Weil experiences the fragmentation of consumerism through the ideal model of the city-state. Writing in Marseilles, Weil found Greek science superior to modern practices because "idea of equilibrium oriented all research towards the good." Equilibrium, like God, is something that exists both inside and outside yourself...

Like the male modernists of her time, Weil was yearning towards a transcendental state of decreation. It's curious how she gets there. Artaud found "cruelty" in the rituals of the

Tarahuma Indians and the dances of the Balinese. Georges Bataille and the College of Sociology studied primitive societies and dreamed of abject human sacrifice. To the intellectuals of Weil's time, influenced tremendously by Nietzsche, Platonism was something that they'd read about a hundred years ago at school; too far beside the point to even be refuted. Perversely, Weil reinvented Greek thought as a struggle for transcendent ethics, value: a moral logic-system, yearning towards "the good," that is large and absolute enough to annihilate merely individual concerns.

In a cranky letter (never published) to the magazine *Cahiers du Sud*, Weil complains that the writing of her time is essentially psychological. And this psychology, she claims, consists of describing states of soul without any discrimination of their value, "as though good and evil were external to them, as though the effort toward the good could be absent at any moment from the thought of men."

Weil uses ethics the way Bataille uses sacrifice, with an Artaudian sense of cruelty: "an appetite for life, cosmic rigor, application, implacable decision, submission to necessity, absolute consciousness…"

"The idea of value," Weil wrote in 1941, "is at the center of philosophy. All reflection that deals with the idea of value… is philosophic; every effort of thought that deals with another object than value is alien to philosophy."

To her, ancient Greece, where all the separate fields of study were *connected* through a search for equilibrium, was a template for utopia. This belief in equilibrium implies that things have value. Therefore, Greek culture has an ethical base.

In her later work, Weil tried to prove that Catharism, an

offshoot of the 3rd century Gnostics, was attempting to expunge the remnants of Judiasm from Christianity and return to western thought's Hellenic base. The triumph of the Romans over Greece signified the Fall of western culture from a unified idealism. This Fall was accompanied by the development of algebra. Geometry required "purity of soul." It was a mapping of God's universe. The hand of the geometer was moving in God's shadow, uncovering spatial commonalties and laws. Whereas algebra ushered in the dawn of signification. It was an abstraction, in which physical things came to be replaced by signs.

Platonic thought was absolute: it left no margin for the kind of intellectual debate that she excelled at. "Simple intellectual curiosity cannot give one contact with the thought of Pythagoras and Plato, because in regard to thought of that kind, *knowledge and adhesion are one single act of mind.*"(*Letter to Deodat Roche*, 1941) Weil blamed the influence of the Old Testament for the violence of this separation. The Old Testament was a document which she, a Jew despised.

The Greeks were sad. Like her, they "kept their eyes open." But their sadness had an object. It was borne of the separation between experience and "the natural felicity of the soul." Reading history as if it were a fairy tale, Weil longed for a return to a vocabulary including words like virtue, nobility, honor, honesty and generosity. She lamented the disappearance of any sense of "value." "The Surrealists have chosen the total absence of value as their supreme value," she moralistically wrote.

She overworked. Years spent shuttling on trains between the deadbeat towns she chose to teach in and trade union conferences, political meetings, writing articles and position papers, refusing to live more comfortably than the poorest workers, suffering these blinding headaches, while continuing her notebooks and research.

She was formidable and ridiculous to her avant-garde contemporaries. While the Surrealists entered "politics" by lecturing on dreams to groups of workers, Weil remained an activist for many years. Her seriousness and argumentativeness, her infatuation with Greek culture, the clothes she wore, her awkwardness and hand-rolled cigarettes, her total lack of interest in relationships or sex, her willingness to project herself so deeply into work that there was no longer any separation between her life and thought, made her an admirable freak, and hence, a target. Briefly, she crossed paths with Laure, the muse and girlfriend of the philosopher Bataille. Laure's reckless tragic life made her an icon of the avant-garde, but unlike Weil, she had no work.

Georges Bataille loved Laure, but Weil fascinated him. Both had voracious intellects, good connections, and interests spanning most areas of the culture. Both were writing towards a spiritual transcendence in relation to their times. For a while they met for lunch at a bistro near the Stock Exchange to talk, exchange ideas. After she died, Georges used his knowledge of Simone to move in for the kill. The character Louise Lazare in Bataille's novel *The Blue of Noon* is based upon his remembrances of those meetings.

It's usually when I'm most depressed that I meet someone who attracts me through an irresistible mixture of danger and absurdity. And then things happen... I don't know if it's me who follows her, or she who follows me. I only know that these situations leave me even more unhappy…

Bataille's "I" in *Blue of Noon* spends a summer bouncing between two Slum Goddess stations on his voyage to depravity. "Lazare" is the talking-whore he lunches with; "Dirty" is the fucking-whore whose room he visits later in the afternoon.

"Usually the girls that I go out with are better looking, better dressed," Bataille writes *a clef* about these lunches with his sometime-colleague. "Her clothes were dirty, they were badly cut, and torn. She had the air of never seeing what's in front of her, she was always bumping into chairs and tables. Her face was sallow…" Pages later, he describes Weil's character as "a dirty hook-nosed Jew." In 1949, writing in *Critique*, he explicitly discussed Weil's work, finding it "odious, immoral, trite, irrelevant and paradoxical."

She never knew when the headaches would begin, and once they started, she didn't know how long they'd last for. Her entire body tensed beyond the point where it is possible to let food in. Sometimes, when she couldn't stand it, she'd recite George Herbert's *Love*, summoning Christ's presence, as if it were a talisman or a mantra –

"And know you not, says Love, who bore the blame?
My deare, then I will serve.
You must sit down, says Love, and taste my meat.
So I did sit and eat."

A SINGLE moment of true sadness connects you instantly to all the suffering in the world. In the world of fairy tales, sadness is redeemed by acts of gentleness and kindness. *Feeling your head exploding, feeling your brain on the point of bursting to bits.* The longer that a person cannot eat, the harder it becomes for her to find the perfect food.

What is a sacrament? The girl's recalling words that come from either poetry or the Roman Catholic catechism. *A sacrament is an outward and visible sign of an inward and spiritual grace.* Aliens & Anorexia. The girl is standing on the highway in the middle of the North Island of New Zealand with her thumb out. Right now she's very sensitized. Not knowing where she'll sleep tonight, she feels the hills wrap round her shoulders like a blanket. There are presences in the landscape and they're speaking to her in a language that she doesn't fully understand. *And the power of Love, which surpasseth human understanding.* Ulrike's and Irena's and Simone Weil's histories were a fairy tale, a joke. The more you think, the more impossible it is to eat. The panic of altruism, tripping out on content, anorexia: all three are states of heightened consciousness, described as female psychological disorders. Does it matter how you get there?

The panic of altruism is something like the panic of starvation. This is what happens inside a person's body when they starve:

In starvation's early phase, known as catabolism, the body realizes it is no longer receiving enough nutrients to sustain itself and responds by trying to tune down. The brain sends messages to the thyroid: slow down! Reflexively, the thyroid takes two actions. It stops producing hormones (sex is secondary to the survival of the organism), and it secretes a chemical, T-3, previously unknown to it, which slows the metabolic pulse by 5 percent.

In phase two, the body starts to eat itself. Fat decreases, protein wastes. *When I starve I feel as if my blood is getting thin*, and this is literally what happens. The body seizes blood's rich hemoglobic protein to sustain its vital organs. When blood's exhausted, the brain then turns to muscle groups and skin. Stripped of all its protein, the skin is rendered dry and thin. The brain turns down the body's heat. The temperature drops.

To assert, as most psychoanalytic literature on anorexia does, that starving girls stop menstruating because they're scared of "femininity," runs contrary to biologic facts. In phase three, menstruation, regulated by the pituitary gland, stops. Reproduction is a luxury to the survival of the organism, which must now conserve its blood and hormones.

Generally, the process of starvation takes about five weeks, although those who are already thin and sickly may die within ten days of stopping eating. In the case of malabsorption, a frequent cause of death in AIDS, starvation's partial and prolonged and therefore lasts a little longer…

Back from NYC yesterday where everything strangely, sickeningly turned. Leaving Jane & Charlie's loft and their children for the library that morning, pale and lemony December light at 9 a.m., a smooth and gliding happiness of being in New York again where people fix you instantly and hard in an impression, nothing escapes anyone and the city is all eyes. On St. Luke Place, the buildings curve around the contours of the street like the buildings near the river in Lyon… but then at 6, going innocently to the party and being pulverized by Sharon's nervousness and Richard's pointless

rudeness... the anxious skepticism at this harmless poetry event is
so thick you can lean up against it like a wall. Particles of fear
that isn't mine begin entering my body, my stomach clenches. Back
at the loft I say goodbye to Jane and then a rat runs out from
underneath my car...

taputaro@ibm.net, 12/11/98 7:14 AM, DH Lawrence

To: taputaro@ibm.net
From: ckraus@pacbell.net
Subject: DH Lawrence

Dear Africa,

So yeah, we're on the couch in this guy's post-divorce Irvine townhouse & he is fingerfucking me 'til I come. The afternoon has shifted from this self-conscious hokey porn to a point of true exhaustion. I close my eyes & come & come. He takes his fingers off my clit & starts using them to fuck my pussy. I close my eyes & come & come. The only way that I can let this happen is by not looking at him – something about him is so cold & creepy & off-putting – but if I close my eyes and lean backwards I can sort of reimagine him through the distance of his arm. This works fine. And I'm so shock-y & so busy reimagining him that I only vaguely start to notice that the pressure in my cunt has turned into a lot, and very hard. I try & go with it. But now IT'S TIME TO GO – THIS HAS GONE ON LONG ENOUGH – and so open my eyes, snap back to see his entire fist shoved up my cunt. And I still had to find my way out of the subdivision, back to Freeway 5.

It occurs to me that this is not a very sexy story. Was reading a strange book about Simone Weil and DH Lawrence in the library this week, this very trippy s/m stuff in his later work mixed up with his ideas about technology and World War I. THAT was hot.

It was good talking to you the other day. What you're doing there sounds so impressive, with all these people, cars and vans.

Did you know that it is possible to make someone come just by whipping them? I've only read about this, have no personal experience of it – hmmmm dot dot dot

HALFWAY OUT the LIE, I stop the car and vomit. Since the age of 21, I've been living with a chronic inflammation of the small intestine known as Crohn's Disease. It is despair that triggers chronic illness, a state quite different from depression. I never know when it will hit, but when it does, my body's pitched into a battle between the inflammation and the desire to stay well. It is a question of control. Sometimes the inflammation wins, and when it does, I lay under it. There is *no vacancy*. Despair arises from the knowledge there is no longer any love or beauty in the world. My lonely friend has AIDS. He has no medical insurance, and I loan him money for a car because I can't bear the image of him sick and riding buses to the clinic. In a rush of gratitude, he invites me round to his apartment and shows me his vacuum cleaner collection that he uses to make a living cleaning houses and *bang*, I'm in the hospital for five days. Porousness equals malabsorption. The body is so fraught with information, it becomes impossible to process food.

From my LA diary –
Los Angeles, sometime in the late 90s –

Third day of being sick with Crohn's Disease, not eating. This is a terrible defeat, it just goes on and on. Normally when I eat, the food just goes right through me, that's bad enough, I mean why bother, every fucking meal just makes me weaker, but now I feel the start of an obstruction, the swelling. If I eat the wrong thing now it will get blocked and then we're off – cramps and fever, vomiting, a week of hospital on IV. I'm already on the roller coaster, just resisting the big dip. Jumpy and alert. Sometimes it's possible to use food as a cure. Small amounts of mushy food can sometimes ease through the obstruction, reduce the pain and swelling. Mashed potatoes gratinée, cuisine *bonne femme*.

There is a can of Campbell's "Home Cookin' Fiesta Soup" inside my cupboard. I open up the can and study it. There are rectangular white cubes which must originally have been potatoes, peas and carrots held together in a gummy broth. The vegetables don't look like they were ever in the ground. Impossible to eat food if I can't picture where it came from. And yet somewhere in the background of my stomach, chest, or mind there is this craving for… nutrition. What if the Campbell's soup suddenly became home-made gazpacho? I can't be sure… Gazpacho's less than perfect because the only tomatoes sold in Southern California are thick-skinned squarish objects wrapped in cellophane. I need food but am rejecting it and everything at the most cellular level. I feel it in my cells: I'm starving. Daily life turns into a terror as soon as you start doubting food –

THE PSYCHOANALYST Johanna Tauber believes that anorexia begins around age two. The pre-anorexic baby tries and fails to form an image of herself that's separate from her mother. Boys usually don't succumb to anorexia, but when they do, it's because their mothers were seductive and controlling. In infant-analysis, Mother equals Food. The anorexic is unable to think past this equation. Therefore, the only way of attaining an adult identity is by rejecting food… (*On The Way To The Self*)

Feminist analysis of anorexia gravitates towards the problems girls confront as they reach puberty. Maude Ellman in *The Hunger Artists*: "It is through the act of eating that the ego establishes its own domain." Nancy Chodorow in *The Reproduction of Mothering*: "Because the mother-daughter relationship remains so fluid and pre-Oedipal, the daughter fails to develop a sense of self that is separate from the mother." Therefore, she stops eating. The most polemically feminist analyses of anorexia nervosa interpret it as an adolescent girl's last stand against the female social role and what it "means" to be a woman. Perversely, all this literature is based on the unshakable belief that the formation of a gender-based identity is still the primary animating goal in the becoming of a person, if that person is a girl.

Susie Orbach and Kim Chernin both believe that anorexic girls regard their mothers' lives with horror. They will starve themselves in order to avoid a female life, i.e., a life that's drained and compromised and stunted. Orbach writes in *Hunger Strike*: "Anorexia is a rejection of the female role, a life in service to the needs of others." Mara Palazzoli, one of the most often-cited specialists in this field, is more specific: "The anorexic wishes to diminish those aspects of the female body which signify potential problems." A.H. Crisp is even more judgmental: "Anorexia relates to a basic avoidance of psycho-sexual maturity."(*Anorexia Nervosa*)

But it is female psychotherapists and recovering anorexics who really lead the pack in nailing down the anorexic girl as a simpering solipsistic dog: Marlene Boskind-White, *Bulimarexia:* "Anorexics have a disproportionate concern with pleasing others, particularly men, a reliance on others to validate their sense of self-worth. They have devoted their lives to fulfilling the feminine role." Anorexics are merely "starving for attention" (Cherry O'Neill, *Starving for Attention*) and "as a group, they are manipulative and deceitful." (Hilde Bruch, *The Golden Cage*)

No one considers that eating might be more or less than what it seems. At best, the anorexic is blocked in an infantile struggle to attain a separation from her mother. At worst, she is passive-aggressively shunning the "female" state and role. At any rate, all these readings deny the possibility of a psychic-intellectual equation between a culture's food and *the entire social order*. Anorexia is a malady experienced by girls, and it's still impossible to imagine girls moving outside themselves and acting through the culture. All these texts are based on the belief that a well-adjusted, boundaried sense of self is the only worthy female goal.

Curiously, Judiasm comes closest to conceiving of an a-personal anorexia through the orthodox belief in *mitzvah*. Food is blessed before it is consumed. The blessing is an affirmation that the food is only good, or holy, when it fuels good deeds by humans.

"Like all the mystics, Simone Weil tells us that it is only by destroying the 'I' that it becomes possible to fully believe in, and therefore truly love, the existence of anything outside ourselves," writes her biographer, Richard Rees. "A common criticism of Simone Weil in France is that she was a masochist who exalted pain and suffering as the supreme values. This is nonsense."

So long as anorexia is read exclusively in relation to the subject's feelings towards her own body, it can never be conceived of as an active, ontological state. Because it's mostly girls who do it, anorexia is linked irrevocably with narcissism. But girls don't make good monsters. Their narcissistic bodily dis-ease is so fragile, shaky, so lacking in a center, that their self-starvation can only be a garbled plea for sympathy and attention. Seven decades later, the female anorexic has no more credibility than Janet's pathetic patient. Female acts are always subject to interpretation. We don't say what we mean. It's inconceivable that the female subject might ever simply try to *step outside* her body, because the only thing that's irreducible, still, in female life is gender.

ALL HER life, Simone Weil suffered viscerally from the collapse of beauty. Without justice and the harmony of social life that it implies, there can be no beauty. Weil realized that the War was the death-knell not just of the Nazi's victims, but of the entire fabric of agrarian peasant life. "Art has no immediate future," she wrote in 1943, "because all art is collective and *there is no more collective life*." Beauty is a certain quality of attention. It is the harmony of chance and of the good. Prefiguring Jean Baudrillard's deadpan celebration of an ecstasy of communication by more than thirty years, Weil wrote in *Gravity and Grace*:

> *The relation of the sign to the thing signified is being*
> *destroyed, the game of exchanges between signs is*
> *multiplied by itself and for itself. And the increasing*
> *complication demands that there should be more signs*
> *for signs… We have lost all poetry of the universe…*
> *Money, mechanization, algebra. The three monsters*
> *of contemporary civilization. Complete analogy.*
> *Algebra and money are the essential levelers.*

As beauty disappears entirely from the landscape it becomes ghettoized in art. HeLLO and WELcome to PacIFic BELL's AUTOmated voiceline. Is it a coincidence that contemporary criticism is obsessed with defining "beauty" as the paramount virtue in a work of art?

From my LA diary –
Los Angeles, sometime in the late 90s –

The more you think about food, the more impossible it becomes to eat.

Staying at my friend Sabina's house last summer, my weight dropped 20 pounds, below a hundred. I stood around her kitchen, studying the food inside her cabinets for days. Anorexia is a violent breaking of the chain of desire. White rice, brown rice, pancake mix. Red beans and granola. Is any of this what I really want? No. Like art, Sabina's food can be subjected to a multiplicity of readings. The food is healthy and attractively displayed and yet I sense it's here for visual reasons, not to be consumed. For six weeks I was starving, I could feel my cells contracting. Starving turns into a panic. My greatest hope is that I might find the perfect food: a freshly picked leaf of red or Boston lettuce, grown in season, lightly dressed in home-made vinaigrette. A single crab's leg served with drawn butter in a dirty waterfront cafe beside a trailer park in Maryland near the bay. Oilskin tablecloths, trashy jukebox, fresh sea breeze.

Has it ever occurred to you that food's intensely social? There is just so much to think about before you eat. The origins of food, the social politics of its production. Its presentation. The presence or the absence of true happiness. In its journey to the table, was this food handled by anyone who cared or understood it? None of these circumstances can be the least bit alienating in order for food to taste good. Food's a product of the culture and the cynicism of it makes me sick.

The entire history of gourmandaise is a history of positing utopia. Cucumber sandwiches, buttered, cut in triangles with crusts removed. When I was young, my father used to make up fairy tales to help me eat. Strawberry shortcake in the month of June, Spring's dampness settled into masses of green foliage, women in print dresses, crisp and not too sweet with fresh whipped cream. Lemon delight and honey pear. Vermouth. The names of colors. When I lived in New York City, I didn't leave Manhattan once for seven years. Bruising easily from malnutrition, I stayed mostly in my apartment, reading books and staring out into the airshaft and dreaming about food. Children playing kickball in the late afternoon, the torn-up yards, the smell of dinners cooking up and down the block, "It's getting late!" corned beef and cabbage. Remembering someone else's childhood as your own. But since food's a disembodied signifier, there's almost something missing, something wrong with the picture. (When I can't eat it's because I feel totally alone.)

To question food is to question everything.

To question food is to recognize the impossibility of "home."

Weil as the *anorexic philosopher*... Though Frederich Nietzsche suffered blinding headaches, *The Gay Science* is not interpreted as a Philosophy of Headaches. Yet Weil's writings are often read as biographic keys. It's difficult to tell, from Kenneth Rexroth's 1957 review of Weil's *Notebooks* for the *Nation*, whether he was reviewing the book, or Weil herself, or the whole phenomenon of anorexic girls. At any rate, he didn't like them. He finds her life "egregious nonsense... a sick kind of agonized frivolity." Weil was "the almost perfectly typical passionate revolutionary intellectual woman...a frailer and even more highly strung Rosa Luxemburg," who "made up her revolution out of her vitals..." Rexroth lays the blame for Weil's unholy folly where it belongs: on two men, the Catholic theologians Father Perrin and Gustave Thibon, who took her seriously. "If only," Rexroth imagines, "she had sought out an unsophisticated parish priest, who would have told her, 'Come, come, my child, what you need is to get baptized, obey the Ten Commandments, forget about religion, put some meat on your bones and get a husband..."

What you need is a good fuck, he said to me.

In *Holy Anorexia*, the scholar Rudolph Bell wants to take the magnificence of the medieval female saints and drag them down to his own level. He does this by conflating them with contemporary teenage girls, who he finds pathetic and ridiculous. St. Catherine, St. Theresa, and Hildegaard von Bingham are all essentially the same; they're solipsistic brats. The collective trans-historic She, the holy anorexic, "emerges from a frightened insecure psychic world to become a champion of spiritual perfection... Her will is to do God's will, and she alone claims to know God's will." The holy anorexic is a manipulative vixen; she "commands the war against her body and therefore suffers deeply at every defeat, whether it is a plate of food she gobbles down or a disturbing flagellation by nude devils and wild beasts. Then with varying degrees of success, the holy radical" – like the newly slender teenage girl – "begins to feel victorious..."

Like witches, or female writers, thinkers, artists, who use the names of others when chronicling their own experience, holy anorexics are not just people to be differed with: they must be despised.

Shouldn't it be possible to *leave* the body? Is it wrong to even try? Hungry yet repelled by food, Weil wrote: "Our greatest affliction is that looking and eating are two different operations. Eternal beatitude is a state where to look is to eat."

The Alien is in my eyes. He's flooding my eyes. He's
completely penetrating me, every bit of me in my eyes.
He's in my eyes, he's spreading into my brain. Oh God,

he's in my mind. He's making me feel things in my body
that I don't feel. He's making me feel feelings, sexual
feelings. And he's there. He's everywhere. My body's
changing.
– David Jacobs, 1988 interview with an Alien Abductee

From my LA diary –
Los Angeles, sometime in the late 90s –

My heart and stomach flip while waiting in the endless
gourmet take-out line at Say Cheese on Hyperion. This is the
third full day not eating… I stare through thick plate-glass
at tureens of baby peas in mayonnaise. Ten bucks a quarter
pound, they're canned. Little bits of foreign cheese displayed
on the top shelf like so many sad specimens. English stilton,
camembert. From the bodies of imprisoned animals to the air-
conditioned case, it's obvious this food was never touched
with love or understanding. The chubby woman up ahead of
me seems to think this food is good. She is luxuriating in the
moment when she speaks her choices to the shop girl, even
though the girl is bored and hardly even listening. I'd hoped
to trick myself to eat by ordering the most exquisite food
but now this place offends me. Say Cheese, Say Choose. She
wraps the names of foods around her tongue, pleased with her
passable pronunciation. Why do I hate everything? The food
here is so vastly overpriced, it no longer smells like food, it
smells like bills and coins and plastic.

If I'm not touched it becomes impossible to eat. It's only
after sex, sometimes, that I can eat a little. When I'm not

touched my skin feels like the flip side of a magnet.

The Alien penetrated me very slowly as we sat together on the bed. (*This is Ulrike Meinhof speaking to the inhabitants of Earth... As the rope was tightening around my neck I lost perception but regained all my consciousness and discernment. An Alien made love with me...*) Uncovering his body takes my breath away. The paleness of it underneath the soft dark hair. The Alien was naked. I had several of my clothes on. We're very still. Fibrational quivers between our bodies in the dark. "This's exactly how I imagined it would be. So smooth." It now becomes possible to say anything. Low voice. "Don't move." "I like to hear your breathing."

Like me, the Alien is anorexic. Sometimes we talk about our malabsorption problems. Everything turns to shit. Food's uncontrollable. If only it were possible to circumvent the throat, the stomach and the small intestine and digest food just by seeing. After several weeks the Alien decides that he will no longer make love to me because I'm "not the One." Aliens spend their lifetimes on this planet testing, searching. They get dewy-eyed, nostalgic about hometown virgins.

I'm in my kitchen making chicken noodle soup for the Alien. It's his fifth day of withdrawal from valium and heroin. He can't walk, can't sleep. I want so much for him to eat. Even though he says he doesn't love me, I can't believe it's true. Therefore, I want to help him. "How about a nice piece of wholewheat toast?" I ask, ladling out his soup. "Don't take offense by this," he says, "but there's something I have to tell you. Your cunt smells bad. If you washed the way you should, I would've done the things to you I do to all my other girlfriends." I gasp. Soup spills. "Sorry," he says. "I guess I should've mentioned it when we were dating."

Food stripped of all its color, nutrients and smells and then reconstituted, like my expensive hair (he loves it), Ravissant Salon, $300, like suburban small town cunts drenched in Massengil.

If I could only eat, a little –

Dear Walter Benjamin,

To take LSD in southern California is not the same experience as smoking hashish in Marseilles in 1939.

Last weekend, Sylvère and I went up to Morro Bay to trip again. We took the blotter acid someplace in the desert. Nothing happened. But when we got to Morro Bay and circled round the parking lot, the acid started kicking in. A sweet and pungent taste of chemical – welcome to the Zone – and then the mucous and dry heaving. Like all the other intellectuals of your time, you thought vulgarity had a certain charm. You hung around the port that Sunday evening looking at the faces of the workers. Ugliness, you thought, can be the reservoir of beauty. In the parking lot at Morro Bay, people in fluorescent clothes were pedaling rented tandem bikes with canopies between the giftshops. There weren't any faces. Just these ugly bikes, and cars and asphalt, and grown up men in children's clothes.

Cars crawled back and forth along the four-lane highway between the parking lot and harbor. After waiting for what seemed forever, we crossed. It was hard to tell the difference between the parking lot and the harbor. There was another string of giftshops, fast food restaurants. We wandered through commercial frontage in search of the "attraction": a few real wooden fishing boats anchored in the chudding bay; a few real fishermen with hip-high waders. But when we got there, the attraction seemed so minuscule and dwarfed. There were a few real fish, flailing on the dock. Death through poison, death through suffocation. Three smoke-stacks from a factory built beside the bay emit "Environmental Gas." Across the harbor, a horde of seagulls perched on Morro Rock. And then you look across the ocean, hoping that your heart will stop at the horizon, but the horizon was obstructed by a solemn row of oil rigs and tankers. We were surrounded on all sides.

Dear Walter, after ordering a dozen oysters at Basso's you were tempted to order every single item on the menu because you liked it so much there. Finally you settled on a pun: "I'll take the Lion Paste!"(Paté de Lyon). Food poisoning never crossed your mind. There's a trailer near my house on Figueroa that sells mariscos. Four people died this week from eating them because they were harvested from toxic algae in the Gulf of Mexico, eight hundred miles away. Two thousand pelicans also died...

Everything seemed so secretly and profoundly hilarious. You were your own best company. Or rather – and here, as always, you are so deliciously precise – you were your own most skillful, fond and shameless procurer of pleasure and sensation. Twenty years ago, the last time I took acid out at Evan's Bay in Wellington, it was like that, too. Even if I wasn't, and will never be, as sensitive as you. "My walking stick begins to give me special pleasure. The feeling of loneli-ness is quickly lost. One becomes so tender, feels that a shadow falling on the paper might hurt it." Even if I could only flash my alligator purse at my deadhead boyfriend and pretend to be the actress in *Pierrot le Fou*.

Fog slams down against the harbor and it's starting to get cold – that cosmetic, California micro-climate kind of chill. We think, Hot Soup! – and sure enough, experience a need and it's already been fulfilled, because behind us there's a Chowder Stand. Inside, a Japanese woman ladles gummy wads of chowder into bowl-shaped styrofoam. The chowder costs five dollars, and everything is as immaculately clean as a San Diego public toilet. The walls and floors are tiled; the glass case is a model city, displaying little bits of food. There are no chairs or tables. Sylvère and I take our styrofoam and plastic spoons and huddle on a backless two-seat bench out on the boardwalk against the cold. The orange bench is ergonomically designed for the consumption of fast food. My stomach roils. Several inches from the bench, a trashcan full of styrofoam and plastic overflows.

I'm feeling sick and teary, so Sylvère leads me to the ocean. The beach is sandy, perfect, curiously unfulfilling. It is the sandy beach of daytime soaps and Malibu, implanted in the dreams of people everywhere, like the purple rose tattoo. "There isn't any beauty anywhere!" I cry. "Because don't you see? Beauty's based upon the principle of exclusion–" and I was gasping like the dying fish for air – "A can only be A if it is not also B, C and D. The global food supply – Hearst Castle – postmodern architecture with all that glass mixed in cupolas and porches – Korean salad bars, forty different flavors of identically tasteless food – it's everything you want, except now you don't want any of it!" – and by this time I was spitting mucous, retching in the sand. The empty sky, the cloying sun, the narrow swath of beach grass separating us from the road... The golden coast of

California now seemed hideously exposed.

Dear Walter Benjamin, Dear Sylvère, do you remember that October, how we took a walking tour in Bourgogne, France? We were following the postcard map of the village *pieton* we'd bought at the cathedral bookshop. Past the town, across the fields and out into the forest. There were men and women picking grapes and picnicking at makeshift tables. The oak leaves had already started turning brown. We were climbing over broken stiles – we'd gotten lost – and ended up in some old woman's yard. You asked her for directions and she took us to the cheese-shed out behind her house. The shed was dark. There were lumps of runny amber-colored cream wrapped up in cheesecloth, set out on ancient wooden benches. The cheeses were of different sizes, formed without a mold and aged for different flavors. You were speaking fast Parisian French, she asked you to slow down. The old woman told us how she made the cheese and then she let us taste it. Everything, the cream the shed the farm, combined into a flavor. And this was food.

Later on, we leave the beach in search of prettiness and lobster dinner, figuring we'll find it at the five-star Inn at Morro Bay. At 3 p.m. on Sunday most of the weekend guests have already checked out. A squad of men – male nurses or security guards? – in gray slacks and cranberry polo shirts patrol the grounds. We nonchalantly make ourselves at home beside the pool, but nothing's right. The swimming pool is situated in between the driveway and the parking lot. It isn't pretty. And then I'm ranting, sobbing, Couldn't they just *try* to make it nice? – but even so, none of the cranberry-shirted guards eject us, 'cause even tripping, as a middle-aged white couple, we don't look out of place. And then the clouds roll in and it's too soon for dinner so we wander in to one of the open empty five star rooms with oceanview to take a nap. But even here, the ugliness is overwhelming: chrome furniture, fake stucco over sheetrock, sprays of rayon bougainvillaea, a grotesquely oversized king bed. We play Three Bears, and then decide to take a bath. There isn't one. For ease of maintenance, there's just a shower, though the right-hand corner of the toilet paper is hospitably turned into a fold. Welcome Guests.

Outside a white van pulls up discreetly by the curb. White plastic vats containing cleaning products? body fluids? are passed between the cranberry-shirted guards, emptied and replaced. The Inn at Morro Bay: Rehearsal for a Hospice; a five-star medical waste treatment plant. Lobster has become unthinkable. How can anyone believe its promises of luxury, when clearly it's designed to process guests like so much waste?

Tiny chunks of artificial butter individually wrapped in plastic shells, spread thinly over bleached and starchy supermarket rolls. Tasteless cultured frozen shrimp. Lettuces kept "fresh" for days and hydrated automatically until the flavor's washed away. The cancerous equality of California. There is no beauty because everyone is garbage. Everything is cynically contrived to promote the rapid flow of capital and waste.

Dear Walter, you vowed to eat a second dinner after finishing at Basso's, no longer fearing future solitude so long as there was hashish in the world. The trance wound down when you stopped to have a final ice cream at the Café Cours Belsunce on rue Cannbière. It wasn't far from where you'd started, sitting at a cafe where you'd gazed upon some wind-blown canopy fringes in a state of amorous joy, realizing that the hashish had begun to work. "When I recall this state," you wrote, "I like to think that hashish persuades nature to permit us that squandering of our own existence that we know in love…"

Dear Walter Benjamin, Cynicism travels through the food chain. To stop eating is to temporarily withdraw from it. Without love it is impossible to eat.

"I HAVE fallen into a kind of abyss in which I've lost the idea of time," Simone Weil wrote to her Catholic friend Gustave Thibon in 1942. She'd left Paris with her parents two years ago on June 13th – they saw notices in the street declaring Paris as an open city. Without even going home to pack their bags, they rushed over to the train station. The last train was full. The Weils lied that Simone's father was the convoy doctor. Guards let them squeeze in among the other standing passengers. They traveled south. Two years later they were still living in Marseilles, waiting, like all the other exiled wealthy Jews, to see which foreign government would sell them visas which they needed to get out.

In Marseilles, Weil studied Sanskrit and Catholicism and wrote the notebooks and the essays which would later make up *Gravity and Grace* and *Waiting for God*. There was no point looking for a job, not even in French-colonized Algeria. The Statutory Regulation on Jews, passed by the Vichy government in 1940, banned all Jews from public service, as well as walking in municipal parks or swimming in the public pools.

Weil's year-long experiment with factory work had left her torn in pieces. "Until then," she later wrote, "I knew quite well that there was a great deal of affliction in the world, I was obsessed with the idea, but I had not had prolonged and first-hand experience of it. As I worked in the factory… the affliction of others entered into my flesh and my soul." Poor health made it impossible to continue, although "labor is consent to order the universe," she later wrote.

The philosopher Simone Petrement, Weil's biographer and friend, recalls that after leaving the assembly-line at Renault, Weil had hoped to augment the experience by doing farm work. But at the time her health was bad and so she took another teaching job in Bourges. In Marseilles, she sensed there might be very little time left to realize her plan.

By this time, Weil was gravitating closely towards Catholicism. A Paris friend introduced her to a Dominican priest and theologian in Marseilles, Father Perrin. Perrin was sympathetic to the Jews in general, and especially to Simone. Perrin adored her. She spoke to him of her desire to share the fate of the unfortunate, this time as a farm worker. Eventually she wore him down and Perrin introduced her to Gustave Thibon, a Catholic writer who owned a farm near Avignon.

Everyone conspired to protect her. She spent the month of August at Thibon's estate, not as a worker but a guest. Weil was disappointed. There weren't any workers in the house so she declined to sleep there. The Thibon family sighed, and fixed her up a little cabin. For a whole month, she was happy. She and Thibon discussed philosophy and read aloud in Greek. All that month she found it possible to eat, and wrote ecstatic letters to her parents in Marseilles about potatoes, eggs and garlic mayonnaise, fresh red beets.

In September, when the southern grape harvest began, Thibon conspired once again to make her happy. He convinced a friend to hire her in Millaine on a grape-harvesting crew. As a friend of the Thibon's, Weil was housed in the boss's dining room. But still, she worked. The days were long, and she wasn't very good at it. It was monotonous and draining. "At the end of the year's work you haven't done anything. But you've survived," she heard the people working next to her complaining. Evenings, she put her cape on and walked outside to smoke and look up at the stars. And it was at this time, resting under vines out in the fields, that Weil began reciting The Lord's Prayer incessantly in Greek. Her charity made her radiant, helping the boss's children with their homework, teaching young grape pickers how to read, suffering headaches and exhaustion but managing to work as hard as other grape-pickers. These facts, elicited from her employers in Millaine by her friends Thibon and Petrement, following her death: a hagiography which might be true.

Still, the harvest ended in October and she failed to find another job. And so she went back to Marseilles and started writing in her notebooks –

"The abundance of what she wrote during the last months in Marseilles has no equal, except for the huge amount of writing she did months before her death in London," says Petrement. "She seemed to be in a hurry, like someone who is about to leave with the presentiment of a probable death and wants to say everything beforehand."

It was autumn, 1941. Jews living in Marseilles were now required to register with police authorities in the south. Weil's brother Andre had left France to take a teaching job in Princeton. He and his wife were in New York, furiously petitioning the US immigration service for visas for his family. Eventually he succeeded, and on May 14, they left.

She wasn't grateful. She agreed to leave only because she'd hatched a plan of forming a cadre of front-line nurses who'd be parachuted back onto the battlefields of France, and mistakenly believed that from New York, it might be easier to implement this plan. As Simone and her parents settled into their uncharacteristically small two-bedroom apartment on Claremont Avenue, she was dreaming about returning to the occupied zone of France. She'd lead a squad of kamikaze nurses who'd jump from planes to treat the wounded at the risk of their own lives. She imagined wounded soldiers whose lives might be saved by immediate medical attention. She imagined the agony of those who died on battlefields without any human care or comfort. Weil's squad of nurses would deliberately elect to sacrifice their lives. Her job description amounted to a self-portrait: "women whose characters were mixed with tenderness and brash determination."

There was very little interest in this project in New York.

And in New York, she was entirely cut off from Europe, whereas the exiled Free French Government, headed by de Gaulle, was then running a shadow government in London, in anticipation of a victorious ending to the war. She started writing letters. If she could be hired by the Free French Government in London, she might convince de Gaulle to institute her scheme.

Weil's strategy was not as batty and improbable as it seems. France was then, as it is now, an oligarchy. At 33, Weil's friends and former classmates at the Ecole Normale were among the younger leadership of the exiled government.

And she was indisputably brilliant, a driven worker. So when she wrote to her former classmate Maurice Schumann, he found a job for her in the communications office. Although he probably never, as she'd wished, discussed the kamikaze-nurse thing with de Gaulle.

Still, she left New York in autumn 1942 believing she was on the way to implementing her scheme. Nine other refugees were traveling on the Swedish freighter. Nights, when the sea was rough and dangerous, she assembled everyone on deck to tell each other fairy tales and stories from their homes.

In London, she met with the French Resistance and begged to be sent to Paris undercover. They thought she must be joking. With her hunched shoulders, jagged curly hair and thick black glasses, she looked like every Nazi's caricature of a kike.

No one in the communications office knew what to do with her. Still, she was a member of the French elite, a fact which at that time bore entitlement. She was assigned an office, and asked to edit memorandums on ways that France's bureaucratic structure might be reorganized, following the war. The question didn't interest her. Or rather, it interested her in the largest and most visionary sense. What gives *any* government its legitimacy? she wondered. In the book that was eventually published as *The Need for Roots*, Weil examines government as a form of managed collectivity. What is it that binds individuals together? She wrote about the nature of good and evil, the metaphoric uses of the sacraments. She was well aware, and had been since she visited Germany ten years ago, that fascism triumphed largely through its emotional appeal for unity and collectivity. Can we devise another form of collectivity, she wondered, which binds without annihilating the presence and the power of the person? Evil, she believed, occurs more easily when the person is deindividualized.

"There is a reality beyond the world, that is to say, outside space and time, outside man's mental universe, outside any sphere that is accessible to human faculties. Corresponding to this reality, in the center of the human heart, is the longing for the absolute good, a longing which is always there and is never satisfied..." Weil wrote in her London notebook several months before she died.

Her headaches, which had abated for awhile, started. In London she ate less and less. She refused rich foods because, she said, in France, they were not a part of children's rations.

The Need For Roots was a vision of cooperative patriotism, in which work would form a nation's spiritual core. "To be rooted is the most important and least recognized need of the human soul. The depopulation of the countryside leads to social death."

She was living by herself in the attic room of a boarding house in Notting Hill. She had headaches all the time, and didn't eat, and hunger catapulted her towards exhaustion. In April she was hospitalized and diagnosed with TB. Tuberculosis was rampant throughout Europe during the 1940s. It was part of the "smell of war-time." Antibiotic treatment hadn't yet come into use, and TB was being treated as it had been for five centuries, with a sanitarium regime of total rest and a diet rich in starch and protein, nearly twice the calories of a normal diet. *When I'm sick it's hard enough to eat 500 calories a day... 2000 is an insurmountable goal.* She couldn't eat it.

On the last page of her London diary, Weil writes

wistfully about symbolic food, foods that are sacraments of tenderness and roots. There were Easter eggs and Christmas turkey, strawberry jam, plum pudding. The panic of altruism, the panic of starvation. "The sustenance that a collectivity provides has no equivalent in the world." She must've felt her cells contracting. Hungry yet repelled by food, she asked the Ashford nurses for some potatoes, not mashed, but *gratinée*: cuisine *bonne femme*, she mumbled, prepared by a French woman, the French way.

On August 22 she fell into a coma. The muscles round her heart were weakened by pulmonary TB and starvation and then her heart stopped beating.

This is Ulrike Meinhof speaking to inhabitants of Earth. You must make your death public. As the rope was tightening around my neck an Alien made love with me. When it becomes impossible to form a group, it may be possible for sexual acts between two humans to facilitate the energy-transmission that is needed to communicate with Aliens. Intersubjectivity occurs at the moment of orgasm. When things break down. *Afterwards the Alien took me to a special planet which belongs to Andromedas. The society there treats time and space with intensity, gentleness, discipline and freedom. Over.*

Georg Buchner's Lenz walked in January through the mountains. *It was cold and damp; water trickled down the road.* Nothing worked. In his madness, Lenz hallucinated the end of Germanic romanticism. *If he thought of another person, or tried to imagine him, then it seemed he became that person.*

On March 22, I was visited in New Zealand by Aliens.

We were shooting the car chase scene of *Gravity & Grace* where Ceal and Dr. Armstrong hear each other's voices in their cars. The scenes were all rainy night exteriors. It was around the twelfth night of the shoot, and by this time everyone was totally exhausted. Sometime around midnight the chain of command began to falter. Delphine Bower and the entire art department stalked off location and went home; Continuity was sulking somewhere over coffee. We ditched the walkie-talkies, started shooting wild. For the next few hours those of us who stayed were all united in this crazy effort. It felt like the idea of movie.

That night production base was Level 3 of the Wellesley Street Parking Garage and around 4 a.m. we went back to the trailer. Craft services was packed and gone. That night we'd passed the hundredth slate; that meant that it was my turn to buy the drinks, "director's shout," and we bought beer at an after hours. We set a dozen folding chairs up around the lighting truck and started drinking. Edith the vegan butch AD was there, and the gaffer Tony Blaine, who the next day would be leaving to go back to jail again for drunken first-degree assault. And Harry Carr, and Jeff Mohapa. Someone took out a nylon-string guitar and some of us knew different songs and stories. Alan Brunton and I swapped lines from French poems we knew by heart. Colleen told tear-streaked Celtic stories. As everyone got drunker, the night broke down into a pea-soup winter dawn. And as the sky turned black to gray I had this vivid sense that we were not alone; that at this moment there were other little groups like ours at other places in the world, and that just by being there together we could reach them. The temporary sense that you're no longer just yourself, you are also other people.

Those who seek out Aliens form groups and give up little pieces of themselves. The empty spaces in each person turn into receptors allowing Aliens to enter through the porous surface of your skin. And later Sylvère told me it was on that night, some 14,000 miles away, that David Rattray died after slipping into a coma.

Two years ago Sylvère Lotringer and I had a near-death experience on a fishing boat in the Arctic Ocean. A storm came up and as the skiff slammed up against each icy wave we watched to see if the funky outboard motor would keep the boat from tipping over. And as we sat there huddling in our parkas I felt strangely calm and giddy, imagining what my two best friends were doing at that moment. Their lives passed before my eyes. I saw them very clearly. And there was something mildly hilarious about this, this simultaneity: that while some of us were pitching around about to drown in Baffin Bay, someone else was sitting at her desk working on her dissertation, and someone else was in her Greene Street kitchen, buttering a bagel. That always at each moment there are all these other lives...

No one bought *Gravity & Grace* that February in Berlin.

Two months later I got a form rejection letter from the nice man at the American Independents cocktail party, and a personal rejection note from the director of the Boston Jewish Women's Film Festival. Shortly after that I showed the movie to John Hanhardt, who was then the film and video curator at the Whitney. He invited me to his office to explain why I'd never be an artist. John said although he found my work "intelligent and courageous," it lacked beauty, criticality and narrative resolution. "Perhaps," he said, "some day you'll make a film I'll want to see." And it confused me, wondering why intelligence and courage were considered negative attributes in female filmmaking. So I decided to stop making art until I found an answer to John's question.

The philosopher Gilles Deleuze got anorexia right (his wife was one) by noting that it isn't anything to do with "lack." "Anorexia," he told his girlfriend and collaborator Claire Parnet, "is a matter of food fluxes. The question is: how to escape predetermination, the mechanical sign of the meal." Anorexia is not evasion of a social-gender role; it's not regression. It is an active stance: the rejection of the cynicism that this culture hands us through its food, the creation of an involuted body.

"Those aliens," writes William Burroughs, "nourish themselves on photosynthesis, so you can see why the scum on top want to hack that up. The whole fucking planet is built on eating…"

Millennial countdown: 377 days to go.
Synchronicity shudders faster than the speed of light around the world.

Strawberry shortcake, mashed potatoes.

GAVIN BRICE

GAVIN NEVER did respond to my December 11 email about the strange book I'd found about D.H. Lawrence and Simone Weil. Perhaps he wasn't really interested in technology. Our relationship was vague, intense and undefined. We'd rehearsed our "first meeting" that would happen in mid-January in Los Angeles on the phone a dozen times.

When I finished writing *Aliens & Anorexia* on the 18th of December, I felt I had to tell him. Like politics, movies are a confluence of money, power, ambition, and the desire to do something good in the world. It is a triumph unlike any other when through this captivating and consuming mix, some remnant of *the good* prevails. I didn't know where he was. His movie wrapped around the 13th of December and I didn't know how long, or if, he'd stay on in North Africa. He said he'd planned to spend a few weeks resting over Christmas at a house he owned on an island near Antigua. I imagined him taking walks and gazing off onto a blank horizon, resting, dozing off in swirls of soft pink sand. Gavin was a postmodern mandarin. He'd bought the house ten years ago, employed a local family to maintain it. This struck me as completely admirable. He was diverting some small swirl of global capital towards the sustenance of island life.

Since we'd never really communicated with each other outside the s/m phone and email game, I wasn't even sure of the propriety of thanking him for his presence in my mind. His presence had become a haunting that I wanted; a Brechtian inner-text to the things that I was writing about dead artists and philosophy. The question burned. Though

Gavin and I had never met, I knew him better than most people that I knew. I wrote the ten-line email twenty times. S/m had been my first experience of sex where the other person holds up their end of the deal. Because the deal has limits. How to make the message personal, while acknowledging he had no obligations? Although knowing him had made it possible to imagine doing this with somebody I cared about and knew. Finally, on December 21 I sent it, not knowing what he'd think or if I'd ever hear from him again. And then I left Roberta's house and other things transpired.

Sylvère came back from Paris after visiting his mother. As usual, he was wearing a home-made money belt sewn by his mother the day of his departure and stuffed with fresh 100 dollar bills. He'd grown accustomed to these gifts, accepting them with a mix of shame and gratitude and generosity... his mother wasn't rich, but providing for him gave her pleasure. So usually he spent the money on symbolic purchases and projects, something of value he could attach her money to. We went upstate to our house in Thurman. This time, his mother's gift of money wasn't mentioned. And this time, Sylvère, who normally saw the purchase of a jacket or a pair of shoes as a lapse into American consumption, was spending money like a gambler on a binge. All week we fought. He was morose, withdrawn and bitter. He couldn't spend the money fast enough. He couldn't talk; denied that anything was wrong.

Snow fell off the powerlines. I wanted us to be warm and winterish and happy. I wore my favorite battered cardigan and watched for winter birds – cardinals, our favorite – and drank hot chocolates at the diner twelve miles away in town.

Four days after Christmas, we got a phone call from my

parents in New Zealand. The inheritance my mother had abruptly, unexpectedly received from a distant unknown relative had passed the California Probate Court. The documents were sealed. My parents were no longer poor. No one had come forward and taken it away. The entire definition of my life had changed. I gloated to Sylvère and wanted him to share the giddiness and freedom. We'd go out to Bolton Landing, drink champagne. He wouldn't budge. I coaxed and tried to make him laugh and teased him but still he moped and screamed at me for criticizing some aspects of the philosophy of Deleuze and Guattari.

The next day I dragged him to Round Pound. We bought some apple juice and cheese at the local store and Sylvère bitterly pulled out another hundred and threw the change at me. We walked for half a mile before I started crying from exhaustion. Trying to pierce Sylvère's unhappiness was hopeless. It was enormous. And I remembered why I'd left him, because it had penetrated me. Sobbing, I tried to play the cop. Was it his work, his daughter? Had something happened to his mother?

And then Sylvère remembered something which he still claims he'd forgot. Which he'd automatically erased from memory. Eight days ago, while he was leaving Paris, watching his mother sew the money-belt and feeling the familiar ooze of complacency and shame, he asked her where the money came from that she deducted for him every visit from the Credit Lyonnais. "Il vien des Reparations," she replied. In French and English, the word was spelt, and meant the same. Since 1993, the German government had been automatically depositing money into the bank accounts of the tiny number of surviving French Jews whose apartments had been seized prior to their deportation…

On January 3, Gavin emailed me:

Just got back to la email me when you get back love g

Except I didn't read it until January 9 when I got back to LA. And then I went straight to the dentist for a root canal down in Tijuana, where I overdosed on Panadol and liquid valium… walking down the Blvd. Revolution that night past the zebra-painted donkeys, looking for a third drug that would help me catch my breath. So it wasn't really until January 12, when the drugs wore off that I emailed Gavin –

Hi Gavin I'm back in LA – my number's 323 779-0562 – talk to you soon xxoo chris

In Terry Gilliam's film *Twelve Monkeys*, the subject James Cole is projected backwards from the future towards a destiny he glimpsed in early childhood. The child James Cole witnesses the airport shooting of a stranger. The scene recurs in dreams. But it's only seconds before his death at an airport three decades later that realizes he's become – or always was – that stranger. *Twelve Monkeys* was inspired by two French experimental films, *La Jetée* and *Sans Soleil*, by Chris Marker. *Sans Soleil* is based on letters written by a documentary filmmaker, Sandor Krasna, as he traveled back and forth between Tokyo and North Africa.

All that Fall while I was living in the house on Seacrest Lane, every time the phone rang, I wondered if the call would be from Gavin. I picked up the receiver listening for the static sound of air passing from antiquated cable into the global net of fiber optics as it traveled round the world. *Hi,* he'd say. *It's Africa.*

The narrator of *Sans Soleil* reads passages of letters Krasna wrote while filming in the Cape Verde Islands of North

Africa: *He contrasted African time to European time... He said that in the 19th century mankind had come to terms with space and that the great question of the 20th was the persistence of the different concepts of time...*

In Los Angeles, I waited. Gavin didn't call.

In Tokyo, Krasna discovers the text of a poem by San Taguchi:

Who said that time heals all wounds
it would be better to say that time heals everything except wounds...
if the desiring body has already ceased to exist for the other
then what remains is a wound, disembodied

Was it possible to mourn the absence of a voice? A voice that wasn't ever even whole, but digitally dismantled, reconstructed?

"If this is to be a story of love," says Avital Ronell about a movie script by Marguerite Duras called *Le Navire Night*, "it is because he says that she was a voice to which one loves to listen. He fascinates, hallucinating her voice." And yes, I'd read the film script years ago and thought about it often. It was the story of a romance conducted *entirely through the phone* when two lines cross accidentally: like mine and Gavin's.

She phones him at the same time as he, in space and time. They are speaking. Speaking... They never stop describing. And at the moment that she speaks, she sees herself. He tells her, put the phone down you your heart... He says his entire body's following the rhythm of her voice. She says she knows. That she can see because she's listening.

hey gavin – I emailed you over a week ago – are you around? – x chris

I checked my email, voicemail, several times a day but still, there wasn't any answer.

When someone disappears and leaves a hole behind, you look for information. **Who Was Gavin?** I entered his name on the Internet Movie Database. I searched the archives of *Variety*, the *Hollywood Reporter*; read microfilmed clippings from the *New York Times* and *Wall Street Journal*. Although there were no biographic features on the career of Gavin Brice, by assembling bits of information I was able to chart his progress over fifteen years from the nether-reaches of "world film" to Hollywood insider. By comparing cross-referenced, interlocking crew lists on the movie database, I learned that Gavin had been tangentially involved with projects or producers surrounding both Duras and Marker. Coincidence accumulated. The missing person is a phantom limb. I tracked down all of Gavin's movies. Gathering information is a provisional attempt at creating a prosthetic. I rented an office in the heart of Hollywood and *it came as no surprise* that one of Gavin's scripts was on the counter at the Hollywood Memorabilia store downstairs. Walking along Hollywood Blvd. past the restaurant Musso & Frank's – a venue Gavin had suggested for a possible first meeting – I glanced across the street. There was an *African Imports* storefront.

I bought a plastic Russian camera and started shooting

places in LA that might be sites for meeting Gavin: the Chinese Good Luck Wishing Fountain, the bar at Hop Louie, a road up in the Hollywood Hills called Brahmin Circle that had a distant view of Griffith Park Observatory.

Once I nearly drove past Gavin's Coastal Canyon house but couldn't bring myself to do it. Instead and in despair, I wrote another email:

To: taputaro@ibm.net, 1/28/99 7:57 p.m.
From: ckraus@pacbell.net

Dear Gavin, There is a Marguerite Duras story called Le Navire Night in which a man and a woman meet when their telephone lines cross late at night. Their first conversation is coincidence – which they contrive to repeat – two disembodied voices traveling through the night. These late-night conversations become central to the female narrator's life – the presence of his voice has entered her field so subliminally – one night without warning he is no longer on the line. His sudden absence hits her like a truck. She is haunted by it. And so, like everything unresolvable, this experience enters the realm of fiction dot dot dot
All I asked was that you would not disconnect without telling me. That is the greatest violence. Chris

Gavin answered this within an hour. His email said that he'd been sick, there'd been a crisis in his family. He was exhausted; he had to place responsibilities above himself and his own personal desires. He hoped I'd understand; he had to stabilize his situation. It might take time, *so please do not expect or wait for me…*

I read his message, stunned and humbled. He was a mensch. I regretted all the information I'd accrued, shamed by my curiosity. To contact him again would be unconscionable. I sent a one-line note of sympathy and started living with the distant hope that someday he would contact me.

Two weeks later, I was having dinner at my friend Gary Wagner's. It was an interesting, congenial party that gelled the way things rarely do in southern California. We were an oddly interlocking group of friends, all of us once total rebels and now employed or half-employed in academic settings. And as the party started winding down someone raised the question of insomnia. The topic galvanized us more than any gossip, and each of us praised the merits of our favorite pharmaceutical.

When I got home alone it was still Sunday night, about 11. I couldn't sleep. And rather than waste another precious ungeneric valium brought back from Tijuana, I thought I'd call the Telepersonals once more and listen to the voices. In order to go on "live" you have to record an outgoing message and so I made one up, remembering all the calls I'd had with Gavin. There are certain words that prod or point to the absence of total vacancy, so *Hi*, I said, *This is Jennifer. I'm a submissive woman and I'd love to talk to somebody who's dominant and alert. Someone who has an expanded sense of play and would maybe like to have some stimulating conversation. So leave me a message.*

I sent it out and started scanning through the 85 male voices of my counterparts, the sleepless eager disconnected lonely. My heart turned over around the middle of the loop when I got to Gavin's –

Hi This is Box 6239 calling from Coastal Canyon.

And I'm single, Caucasian, in good shape, well traveled,
articulate, creative... Like to know who's out there
who likes to have FUN...

I played the message over seven times. Of course I wouldn't answer. His right to do this was the same as mine. It didn't matter if he was on the line as an alternative to St. John's Wort or Xanax, or if he was looking for a new life partner. But as I hit the replay button "3", experiencing this rush of altruistic panic towards him over and over, the sweat, the sharp regret, dozens of horny guys were leaving messages in my own box for "Jennifer."

Eventually I played them. The last was Gavin's.

Hey Jennifer – his voice was warm – *It's Gavin in Box 6239. And I'm dominant, and love to play, and would love to talk to you on the telephone. And I find submissive partners enormously erotic to play with. And uh* – and here his voice took on the unpremeditated, assertively self-effacing quality of the greatest actors – *I'm very intelligent, well-traveled, articulate, creative, and your word, I love, "alert", ...So I think we'd have a lot of fun. And uh, please get back to me.* And here I felt him search for something that would make her answer: *And, uh, I really love the sound of your voice.* He paused. *So ... You sound like you're strong, know what you want, and that's VERY EROTIC when you're being submissive. If that makes any sense. So get back to me.*

He didn't recognize my voice. It was like the final scene of *Naked Lunch* by David Cronenberg, in which the armored hearse approaches the border of Annexia. The nightmare begins again before it's even over. For five days I wondered what to do with this. On Thursday night I left for a workshop in Key West, met someone on the plane, and never got there. For the first time in six months I had real sex with a person who I knew that I would see again. When I got home, Gavin's spell was broken. But I still felt terrible regret. The passion of the fairy-tale; *the urge to make things right.* I couldn't bring myself to think of Gavin as an asshole. And so I emailed Gavin once again, disclosing "Jennifer's" identity. And it was weird and creepy – but still the correspondence that we'd had all Fall had touched me very deeply – and I wondered if we couldn't meet just once so I could put a person to this voice that had affected me. I didn't want to write the whole thing off as cynically fabricated intimacy, a cheap aid to getting off. Perhaps we could meet sometime at a coffeeshop and have a chicken salad sandwich?

He never answered. I called the Telepersonals Chat Line this afternoon. Seven months later, Gavin's message is still there. In fact, according to the automated voice, *This person is still a member but is not on the system at this moment. The last time this person was on the system was* – This morning.

At the opening of Chris Marker's *Sans Soleil*, the narrator states: "I've been around the world several times, and now only banality still interests me."

GRAVITY & GRACE

Part 1: New Zealand

Big Picture involves escape from the planet by a chosen few. The jumping-off point is Wellington, New Zealand.

> – William S. Burroughs
> *The Western Lands*

COUNTDOWN. Ticking of a time bomb. The world explodes.

Garden songbirds chirping in the darkness. Fade up on a vegetally radiant suburban lawn.

A topographical map of the southern sector of the city depicts its bombing targets. Airport, major arteries and roads. In the Middle Ages, battle maps were commissioned by the king to commemorate the victories of his army. Tiny figures shooting bows and arrows. Canons strapped to ox-drawn carts. History, barely visible but shuddering underneath the translucent skin of the present.

A hastily dug bed of pink tulips quavering in the wind.

CEAL DAVIS is digging a hole in the lawn of her Remuera home with a pickax. Obviously, she knows nothing about gardening. She is trying to plant a dozen bulb tulips that are already in full bloom. The house behind her is large and gracious, a neo-Tudor of the 1920s, pavilion architecture of the early suburbs. The house doesn't seem to be a vital part of her identity. Neither is it estranged from her. It's just a house.

Ceal Davis is a woman in her 40s. She is one of those women who will permanently evade middle age, a slightly battered cockroach, mutating out of girl to older girl to old. I think she's beautiful. Her blue sleeveless sun-dress lights up her dark-blonde hair and grey-blue eyes. There is tremendous knowledge and compassion in her face; optimism against all evidence to the contrary.

Ceal is planting full-grown tulips in her yard because she has been told to. That is, her dead father appeared to her in a dream and told her to plant tulips. It is the first time he actually spoke words through the flood of serotonin images that have been waking her for months, and Ceal is eager for advice.

When her father died she thought she was prepared for it, but wasn't. Her father was the only person who she knew who fully shared her pleasure in ambivalence. She thinks she's failed him. And now there aren't any older people in her life, and two months ago the literacy program she was running in South Auckland was phased out. Unlike her Remuera neighbors, Ceal has no children and the program was a shred of everything she'd hoped to do, the last thing she wholeheartedly believed in.

Edward, her husband, doesn't know what to do with her. Cancer-ridden parents die. They didn't need the income from her job. Change, he says, is opportunity. She could travel, write her Phd, but she just looks at him and laughs.

Edward watches Ceal tear up their lawn from the upstairs bedroom window. He has never known anyone to be so unconsolable. Tonight he'll be in Singapore for a conference on environmental law. Finally, he shrugs and calls across the yard to her – "I'm off. I'll phone you from the airport."

Ceal snaps to; maintains. She waves and smiles convincingly. "Okay, good luck!"

Stealthily, she counts the paces that will bring him to the taxi. Lately, Edward has become a barrier to the communion she's been entering with her father. She pats the tulips in the ground, there, it's done. She remembers something that she read about the Shakers, how they spoke to all the plants they sowed and wished them well.

The tulips die while Edward's plane is still somewhere above Australia.

CHANELLING BEATS waitressing, Deirdre Saxon thought happily.

She is about three quarters through a routine that lasts six hours, minus lunch break – the part in which she leads everyone down into the Memory Cave to find their birthright – "…And the cave is dark. It welcomes you. You stumble in the darkness, you feel fear." She herself remembers something about the story of Persephone, being kidnapped – the chanting helps put people in the mood.

Twelve women of all shapes and ages are sitting crosslegged on the floor of the Remuera Anglican church hall. Ceal Davis is among them.

"Now, there's a light shining from a room downstairs. You're drawn to it, but your legs are heavy –" Deirdre still considers herself an actress. She has a kind of majesty. Today she'll clear a thousand dollars, enough to pay her rent and fix the crankshaft in her shitty car. Most of the other actresses Deirdre went to school with now work as therapists and publicists. Channeling is proactive. It gives her weekdays free to do auditions and attend rehearsals in the event she's ever cast.

The woman on the end in cashmere sweats is staring at her. It's not unusual for people to break down, but this woman is unusually alert and self-possessed. The others are all deep in trance. Deirdre tries addressing the remainder of the Hero's Monologue to her: "Now, you may choose to leave now, or you may try and mount the stairs." The woman flashes back the wisp of a sad smile.

Deirdre has to deal with this. "You have a *choice*," she repeats, touching Ceal on her left shoulder. "But I don't want one," Ceal replies. "Try not to be afraid," Deirdre oozes. "I know these things bring up – feelings."

But Ceal does not break down. She gets up and changes, leaves and throws her gym bag in the car. "Feelings." It was a joke to come here. Stupidity upsets her more than anything because it implies a poor quality of attention. "Feelings." She feels annihilated by this blowzy woman. If people aren't willing to receive new information there is no point to anything. Feelings are shit, Ceal smiles, feeling powerful and wild. The real trick is to disappear. She thinks she'll take a drive.

MAIN STREET of Otahuhu, bloody sunset going on behind the palms.

The radio inside Ceal's nice white car is tuned to

WNCN, the Concert Program. "Antonio Vi-val-di," the male announcer states in overeducated tones, "His Mag-nif-i-cat, here on WNCN." Her car clips past the rundown blocks of flats, the burger bars, the used appliance storefronts. Ceal trips out on contrast, takes this in.

When the Literacy Project was defunded everyone expected she'd stay on and look for ways of raising private money. *Let this country just become what it deserves*, she sighs. The tiny residential bungalows on Otahuhu's back streets, built in the 1930s as state housing, now sold off to investors and rented to the poor –

And we are to hear the Scherzo B flat minor opus number 31 of Frederick Chopin. Chopin was accused of borrowing scherzos from Beethoven, and though the word 'scherzo' really means 'joke,' most of Chopin's were not so very happy – Ceal can't stand listening to this man's smug voice. She flips the dial.

Last rays of daylight piercing through a stockade fence. The voice of Andre Gregory, noted actor and director: *I guess I start with the journey of the individual into themselves*, Yes, and isn't that the problem? Flipping backwards to the Concert Program, the opening four bars of Bach's *Partita in B minor* cut right through her, bring her back to Blue Alert.

The sky gets dark. It's nearly midnight. Ceal's been driving randomly a long time. She parks the car in central Auckland near the wharves. She walks. She cuts across the bus terminal, headlights of the last bus crawl by. She's still listening to the Bach *Partita*, performed by cellist Ute Uge, each swipe across the instrument's four strings is registering through her body as an act of recognition. She thinks about a poem Anne Waldman wrote called *Girls*:

If you live by the water, Gabrielle
you lucky person
If you live in a forest, Evelyn
Or deep in a valley Maureen
High on a mountain, Janine
Are you closer?
Tell me, are you closer?

4 o'clock in the morning
A motor idling despondently
outside a chicken takeout joint across the street
I hate it, girls
I hate that motor

A string of colored Christmas lights outside the Terminal Cafe blink off and on. Ceal thinks she'll have a cup of tea. She joins the balding late night proofreader poking at his eggs underneath fluorescent lights and starts scratching in the diary she's been carrying with her everywhere these four months. Travel posters advertise vacations in the sun. *I write these things down so someone else can read them at the end of the world...* Ceal sips her tea and sighs.

IT DIDN'T take Max Bochner long to ditch the people from the Goethe House. They were embarrassed by the turnout for his reading, although he didn't care. The entire Australasian tour was being paid for by the DAAD as some kind of payback to his publisher. Next week he'd be in Tokyo. Despite the thin first-world facade of downtown highrises, IBM and Infotech,

New Zealand mostly reminded him of traveling in Bavaria before the Wall. Clearly, they weren't ready for his latest book, *The Toilet*.

He walked around Karangahape Road and ended up downtown at the Auckland Intercontinental. Amongst the business types gracing the Piano Bar there were two girls who looked like cartoon whores. Probably students at the local art school. He wondered if performance art had reached New Zealand. Had high-strung girls progressed from throwing pots to sticking root vegetables up their anuses?

Grace, the long-haired girl was some brand of Polynesian, very pretty. The short-haired one looked troubled, generic-punk à la early Kreuzberg. She said her name was Gravity. The two mistook him for an easy hit and this amused him.

Long before last call it was decided that they'd all go back to Max's. Grace reached underneath the table towards his crotch while Gravity gathered all her nerve to ask him for 300 dollars. She must've upped the price when he told them he was staying at the Pan Pacific. Translating marks to dollars, he found this totally acceptable. Max liked watching amateur pornography: the way the person's face zoomed in and out behind the mask of sexuality. If he could get the pretty one to suck his cock, okay, but then again it might be interesting to watch the two of them go at it, especially since this may not have yet occurred to them…

Staggering up the hotel promenade, the drunken girls are shouting out the chorus of some artschool song, ah youth –

> *Expression is a metaphor*
> *Repression is reality*
> *Relations are all fetishized*

Except for bestiality

Was sheep-fucking a national trope? Yesterday morning on the plane two guys from Animal Husbandry sprayed the entire fucking cabin with insecticide.

Arm-in-arm, the three stumble through the fern and marble atrium. A powerful looking woman in a well-cut suit strides past, trailed by a clown dressed in his Sunday suit who's obviously begging.

"We lead the Pacific Rim in corporate giving." The woman's voice sounds like a kindergarten teacher overdosed on Xanax. "But giving is a partnership." The clown doesn't seem to understand. He nips along, crazed and desperate.

Max remembers a joke he heard that evening at the Goethe House about this very subject, sheep-fucking. "Hey," he says, "You'll like this. Have you heard the one about the sheep in Te Kuiti? You see, I'm heading down to Te Kuiti in my car, and I see this guy fucking a sheep. What kind of bloody town is this? I thought. And I drive along a little more, and sure enough there's another farm, and there's another farmer, ramming it up the ewe. Well I get to the third farm there's a fellow leaning on a fence just pulling on his thing – that's strange –"

The corporate princess and her jester clear the automatic doors. Now she is regretting this. "You see," she tries explaining patiently, "an Extraterrestrial Institute just will not enhance the image that we're trying to convey." She wishes that the valet guy would hurry. "Read the annual report!" she says. "We fund sports, we fund indigenous handcrafts, we fund ballet –"

Dr. Thomas Armstrong is genuinely confused. She knew

what this was about. They'd spoken on the phone, she must've read his 20 page proposal.

"And so I go into the nearest bar and ask what's going on here?" Max steers the girls over to the bank of elevators. "Oh, the barman says, that last one will be Tom. And why is he pulling on his strudl thing? Because, the bar man says, he's too cheap to get himself a sheep!"

The woman in the suit smiles coyly. "Didn't you enjoy the dinner? I just wanted to meet someone who believes in UFOs." Finally, a black sedan pulls up along the roadway. She lunges for it, leaving Thomas Armstrong in a state of humiliated wonder. Is he a freak? He runs awkwardly behind her car. "Then buy me! Put me in a cage! I'm not a beggar!" And now he's screaming. "Forces here are gathering and there's nothing I can do to save you!"

Back inside, the girls prod and poke and laugh. Max wonders if there's something he's not getting.

The car turns right on Mayoral Drive disappearing down the hill into the city. Greed and evil. Thomas may be powerless against the city as it stands, but still, he has this knowledge. His voice cracks a little as he yells –

THE FUTURE IS NOT IN OUR HANDS

– to no one in particular.

Back at the Terminal Cafe, the egg man's gone. Ceal's tea is cold. And yet she stays, because everything that's happened since she started driving has carried the most peculiar charge...

GRACE WAS the one who looked as if she'd had a blissful

and untroubled childhood, although it wasn't really true. At 53, her mother was now living in Coromandel with a boyfriend who was maybe, 24? She didn't really know her Maori dad, or any of his family. The past two years at university had been her longest time of staying still. Gravity sometimes tried convincing her that this escort/hustle plan was a way of working through her ambivalence about her mother's promiscuity. More likely it was a way of working through her ambivalence about Gravity. Gravity always had a plan. Reckless actions fueled by convoluted logic. Gravity was driven, though to nothing in particular. This excited Grace, who in her heart knew better. Grace thought she could protect her.

The German man is pouring out three whiskeys neat and taunting them with some sexual innuendo he obviously mistakes to be above their tiny heads. He had a balding oblong head and bow-shaped legs. Earlier that night while they were getting dressed at Grace's flat they'd figured out a new routine: Grace would come on very sexy, flashing hair and tits, and Gravity would stall the action with a story. "Trust me," Gravity had said.

So when Max tells them how he likes to "watch," Grace shudders, but Gravity jumps in: "But do you like to listen?"

"Sure," Max says, waiting for a dirty story.

"Right. What's sex without communication?" Grace deadpans.

The two girls are alike enough that they can totally confuse him. Just when it seems like Gravity's in charge, Grace steps in. She takes her shirt off and reaches coyly towards his cock and banters back and forth with Gravity about fiction, voyeurism, Goethe and adrenal glands.

Sometimes they get onto this plateau where they can be each other and themselves, together in a single moment, which is much more than being one.

This is the part that Grace likes best, though Gravity is more intrigued by what happens to herself with all the men. Is she turned on by this? Yes and no. There is this character she's creating and it isn't really her and she's curious and angry at just how well it plays with all the men. It's like a confirmation of how despicable she really is to them. When she looks at Max she makes her eyes get very wide. Once when she was trying this alone she'd actually let one of the men fuck her. He kept pushing, pleading, begging, and finally he'd worn her down. She wasn't having sex with anybody real and all this groping turned her on, a little, so she'd let him. She felt ashamed for giving up control but the fuck itself was surprisingly benign. She'd never mentioned this experience to Grace, because she only wanted Grace to see her certain side.

"Once upon a time," Gravity begins. There is this fairy tale she's read that she always knew somehow she would use, about the gift of waiting. Let the assholes wait. A princess and six brothers, charmed by a wicked stepmother into toads. The princess' task: to set them free by weaving shirts from sea anemones, maintaining total silence.

"Rub my cock," Max whines.

"Hang on Max, we're getting to the moral, the climax of the story," Gravity replies. "To act is never difficult. It's much harder to do nothing at all!"

She nods to Grace who grabs her shirt. In two seconds flat the girls are out the door.

CEAL LOOKS up and out across the empty bus depot at the Terminal Cafe.

Tempered by this new defeat, Thomas Armstrong gets into his tiny car and drives downtown. As he passes the Cook Street entrance to the Pan Pacific, two girls rush out onto the sidewalk, laughing, holding hands, running parallel to his car.

MEET ME ON THE ASTRAL PLANE –

Yellow streetlights in the city shimmer.

Ceal is driving. This time, she feels impelled. She takes a left on Albert, right on Swanson, heading towards the vicinity of the hotel.

Thomas thinks he's hearing voices. The voice he's hearing sounds like Ceal's: *Hosanna and I say unto you, the people of the earth are rushing towards suicide in great numbers!* He takes a right on Wellesley, left on Albert.

Thomas's voice is echoing around the inside of Ceal's car: *The world's mind is in lethargy. It does not want to awaken!* The car is stuttering underneath the strip-lit office blocks, past drunks and all-night parking –

– He takes a right at the corner of Victoria, circles Albert Park to Princes Street – he is guided now not just by voices but by signs: American Express, the first four letters dimmed, *ICan Express* – the words *Peace Infomix* stand out in red above a building east of him on Grafton Road – *We are the final generation*, Ceal's voice intones.

Ceal swoops north on Fort Street, south on Princes, east

on Symonds. The voice inside her head shoots through her fingertips and guides the wheel – We are the final generation – it's like the sense of possibility that's been sucked out of the urban landscape has been rewired into two giant blue electric signs – *Peace Infomix* – her car is moving towards them –

But as she turns the corner onto Grafton Road, her white car falters and the voices stop. She's out of gas. She steps out into the night, directly underneath the signs but now there's nothing but the sound of crickets. She is totally abandoned. At least two miles to the nearest all-night petrol station, there isn't any other traffic, she pulls her jacket tighter round her shoulders, holds back a sob.

Tiny yellow headlights round the corner of Symonds Street onto Grafton Road. A man gets out. "You need some help?" he asks.

His voice is the same voice Ceal was hearing in her car. Does she need help? "Yes, I do, of course I do –" and Thomas recognizes her voice too – "We all need help." He clasps his hands around her shoulders. She has this sense of coming home.

"I'm Thomas Armstrong."

"My name's Ceal."

Two bodies, small and spinning underneath the lights of Newton Bridge, *Peace Infomix* above them. Sound of foghorns mixing with a late-night saxophone.

LATER, SITTING in an all-night bistro near Herne Bay, Ceal feels like she can tell Thomas everything. The fact that someone's listening makes it possible to find words. Above their booth, in the place where the jukebox ought to be, there is a painting of Mt. Rangitoto, the dead volcano that sits in Auckland harbor that erupted 700 years ago, or could it be the future? The mountain's single crater head spewing balls of fire down into the ocean –

Ceal is almost coy and girlish.

"All spring," she says, her index finger making little patterns in the melting candle, "I've felt on the brink of something, like something's catching in my throat. There's an incredible sadness, but it's a good sadness. I don't want it to go away."

Thomas seemingly dismisses this. "I wouldn't make too much of it." She cringes, is about to back away.

"The sadness that you feel is just a threshold. Not everyone can get there. Right now you're very sensitized. Something is awakening in you that goes back beyond your life to things you've long forgotten. But don't get stuck. You have to use it now to reach the other side –"

And she considers this. It is the first time in recent memory that anyone's suggested something new. She wonders if her father's voice, his message to plant tulips, had anything to do with this.

Thomas has no doubt it does: "Something else is trying to get through."

She hesitates, thinking about the channeling fiasco.

"Well, I don't know."

"The Institute I represent is charting ruptures in the atmosphere. There's going to be a big change in the earth's surface very soon –"

"Are you a scientist?" Ceal retreats politely.

"No – I'm actually a doctor with the University Student

Health. But the voluntary nature of our institute enables us to tell the truth. You see, these vibratory beings that you seem to be aware of – it is essential that we contact them."

His intensity amuses her. And yet what happened was extraordinary, a kind of evidence that impresses her because it was so unexpected and against her will.

"I don't know what you're asking me," she stalls.

"I think you do."

AND THEN he takes her to a laboratory hidden underneath an empty warehouse. The entire ERG – Violet, Betty, Bob, Irene and Lee and Harold – are hard at work in a room crammed full of oscillators, charts and graphs and pickled fetuses. They are the nerdiest collection of suburban aunts and uncles Ceal has ever seen. Priorly, Ceal has regarded the obese, the acne-ridden and the mad with the sympathy that comes from being separate from them. She screams.

The next morning she wakes up late, deciding not to think about this. She goes downtown to do her hair. The receptionist tells her that her colorist's running late and offers her a manicure. She pages the beautician, and out steps Betty, the fat lady in the polyester pants suit from the ERG.

Betty reaches greedily for Ceal's hands.

"Hello, Ceal," she beams.

AND SO Ceal yields, and cautiously becomes the mascot of

the ERG. Thomas, it seems, was right about her sadness and her dreams, to see them as a conduit, because a few days later when Ceal was upstairs writing in her notebook she felt the force of something move her hand.

"My–name–is–Sananda. The cares of the day cannot touch you. Be patient and wait for I will come soon."

Ceal knows nothing about automatic writing. She has never wished to be a Surrealist in the Paris of the 1920s, dreaming fabulous constructions through the Nap Period of Robert Desnoes. She watches her right hand as if it's not a part of her. It moves. The movement grips her with a panic, as if she's filled with something that she doesn't want to lose.

At first the messages are faulty. She doesn't question what they mean, or if "Sananda" is a metaphor. Thomas is ecstatic. It's as if the past four months were a kind of hibernation, preparing her for this more active state. Sananda's messages describe the twin planets he inhabits, Clarion and Cerus. Some days, even when she's sitting with her pencil and her notebook, there aren't any messages. Ceal trains herself to wait.

In the middle of November, Ceal receives a message from Sananda that he is now prepared to meet with her and Thomas and the others. The script curls around the "t" in "meet" and then breaks off. Where? Ceal wonders with her body until the clenching of her fist relaxes and the letters spray across the page –

"Next Saturday."

But where? – the question pounds around her head until Sananda moves her hand to form the words –

"In the Rugby Park. At Bloodworth Field."

NOVEMBER 26 – THE FIRST TRIAL

And so on Saturday morning, Ceal and Thomas, Violet, Betty, Harold, Bob, Eileen and Lee arrive at Bloodworth Field in Ceal's white car. Eileen's prepared a picnic. Bob's brought along his camera. Betty hands out seven pairs of special sunglasses that will protect them from the atmosphere's negatively ionized rays. Visible from most parts of the city, dead Rangitoto slumbers in the distance. It is a sunny cloud-streaked late spring day. There isn't anything to do at Bloodworth Field but eat and talk, so Thomas spreads a blanket and that's what they do.

Hours pass. Satiation segues into lassitude, shot through with little pinpricks of anxiety. Eileen puts away the picnic things, and everybody puts their glasses on. They sit cross-legged in a circle staring at the sky towards Clarion and Cerus like a dog pack baying at the moon.

By 3 o'clock they're foraging through the remnants of the picnic basket. Violet munches bitterly on one of Eileen's apples. She's never liked this woman Ceal. Bob is bored. Lee, Eileen's half-wit heavy-metal son, pops bubbles in the sandwich wrap. Ceal is acutely aware of everybody's mood. "You know," she whispers guiltily, "the message didn't say a time." Even Thomas puts away his special glasses. But then Ceal sees a figure walking towards them far across the field.

It is a man in black. Gaunt, 6'4", black overcoat, long gray-black hair. "Look!" Ceal cries. She hears vibrations in the air.

Ceal searches for a gift – a water bottle from the picnic basket – and runs across the field to meet him. Eileen reaches to protect her: "Stay back, the man looks crazy."

"No," Thomas thunders, "let her go!"

When Ceal reaches him she feels his energy shoot through her. "Would you like a drink?" she offers shyly. The man says No. He walks away, and loss floods through her. She runs back over to the group. "The melon – the melon – where's the melon?" No one can find it, so she and Lee run to check the car. He searches through the trunk and tosses Ceal a small rock melon. Blind instinct pushes her towards the man's ever-shrinking figure. He is walking towards a catacomb-sized sewer pipe cemented in the wall along the hill. The sun is dropping fast behind the hill, it's difficult to see him, and when Ceal squints past the sun the man is gone.

Back on the picnic blanket, not everyone's convinced. "But Sananda promised us a spaceship," Harold mourns. "Don't you see?" Thomas asks him, gathering conviction, "It's a test. They're showing us the limits of our expectations." "I don't know," Eileen complains, "they let them out of hospital too soon."

Ceal stands alone out on the empty field, gazing off into the sewer. Her frail figure moves Thomas to a new conviction. "Words cannot explain this!" he exclaims.

Ceal stands dead still, proffering the melon, her orange sundress shifting in the breeze, as expectant as the Andrew Wyeth painting of Christina on the hillside. She is immeasurably moved.

"WE'RE NOT escorts or anything. We're students," Gravity explains.

She has parked herself beside an off-duty detective in the

lounge bar of the Carlton Arms. Grace, according to their plan, is hanging round the bar and flirting with half the Parnell rugby team. Grace looks hot – a tiny black slip dress, long black hair skimming round her naked back and shoulders. Gravity the prim-procurer guides the man to get a better view. "Grace," she says, "is Maori." But race gets no reaction. Gravity tries again. "She's new in town." Still, the man says nothing.

Gravity wonders if he's stupid or he's fucking with her. "We like to meet people," she says slowly. "You know – have a good time?" He nods as if he finally gets it. "My father is American like you." The shadow of a thought moves across his face as he looks at her incredulously. She takes it as a sign of interest. "Perhaps we could – go up to your room? You could show us what you like to do?"

Finally he smiles. "Do you know who I am?" She doesn't. "I could have both of you arrested. But I won't."

Minutes later the man is on his knees upstairs, his bald head bobbing under Gravity's long skirt. Gravity thinks this is a great adventure. The man has a handlebar mustache. It tickles. Gravity tosses back her head, fakes a moan and winks at Grace, who is sitting on the bed and flipping a remote and at this moment would rather be anywhere than here.

SO THE next day when they're walking up to school and Gravity is gloating about all the easy money, Grace practically explodes. This is so fucked up, being used by Gravity as her double to work out something that's unnameable and twisted and doesn't have anything to do with her. But since she's let it go this far she is a part of it, and now she can't say anything because to say it would be saying everything and so she just says No, and sometimes a bitter, Yeah.

They pass a beautifully dressed older woman handing out some nutty leaflets in the mall. She doesn't look like a Jehovah's Witness. "Read about the flood! The flood is coming!"

The woman's Ceal.

Gravity grabs one of Ceal's pink leaflets from Grace's hand, crumples it and cracks a joke. God, Grace thinks, sometimes Gravity is just so full of shit, it's hard to even look at her.

Ceal's voice carries down the outdoor mall. "We have the teachings that will save you! Read about the flood!"

Gravity feels terrible. She feels the weight of everything that Grace's not saying and if she can't still be the ringleader of their friendship then who will she be? She feels something coming up she can't begin to talk about. "Listen," Gravity says, "I don't think I'm gonna make the Anthro scene today. Call me out at Lindsay's?" Grace barely notices her stalk off.

"We have friends," Ceal cries, "on other planets."

Grace wonders what it is about the woman's presence that is so much more compelling than her apocalyptic rant. She circles back and takes another leaflet. Grace thinks, the only crazy thing about this woman is her words.

REINA WHAITIRI'S videotaped lecture about the 19th century Taranaki prophet, Te Ua is already underway when Grace creeps in 15 minutes late. The students hunch heads down writing in their notebooks. Already, a haze of languor hangs over the room.

Not much is known about Te Ua. We can guess, though, that he wasn't widely respected by the people of Taranaki. Forty years old, no known property or children, he virtually lived as a hermit.

Reina Whaitiri is about Ceal's age. She has a broad strong face, long hair streaked with gray. Unlike Ceal, she radiates this sense that she belongs somewhere. She is a woman, not an older girl. Grace feels that Reina Whaitiri must be speaking to her. She's more aware than usual today that she is the only Maori student in the room.

But when the Land Wars spread, Te Ua fervently believed he was chosen for a vision. The world would end by flood, but his people would gather on a hillside. When all the Europeans drowned, a glorious prehistory would begin again.

"Read about the flood." Grace takes another look at Ceal's pink leaflet. And wasn't Te Ua's crazy vision of defeat the same as Ceal's?

AND NOW that Gravity's decided not to go to school the day seems long and pointless. It's a 45 minute bus ride home, and at any rate, home is too depressing: a tiny bedroom in Lindsay McGoren's New Lynn bungalow, where he lets her live rent-free, in exchange for cleaning once a week and listening to his pathetic made-up stories about the junkie glamour scene in London. At least he's never tried to fuck her. Gravity wishes she was gay.

She heads downtown and underneath the former Railway Station through the tunnels. There's no one here. Somebody's spray-painted the outline of Rangitoto on the wall, the dead volcano, *City of Volcano, Static 98*. She remembers how she used to throw her voice around between the hills when she was growing up outside of Palmerston, how it came back to her. And so she tries, a little shy at first, sending out her voice around the tunnel. It echoes back. And then she runs through all the notes from high to low until she's screaming, and when she can't scream any louder, she kicks the wall. Harder, faster, 'til it really hurts. She wants to get this pain out of her body. But nothing changes and the wall's still there.

SUNDAY AFTERNOON *at Ceal's:*

Ceal's leafleting has brought in five new members to the ERG: Clifford, a Chinese history student; Raeleen, Bob's gearhead girlfriend; Arthur, a junior lecturer at the university; Susan, a kindergarten teacher, and Grace, who is traveling incognito with a huge tape recorder in her bag. Grace wants to infiltrate the group as a participant observer. She'll write an anthropology report contrasting the tragedy of Te Ua with these white suburban goofballs called *When Prophecy Fails*. No one suspects Grace of anything. She seems like such a lovely girl.

Since the magic night when his car and Ceal's collided,

Thomas has watched events escalate according to a larger plan that far surpasses any precognition. The meeting at the rugby park set off a new burst of communications from Sananda: confirmations of the flood, and even promises of conveyance to another world. Sometimes Thomas wonders if he's ready. For all these years of study, he's never experienced so much as a sighting of an interplanetary being before.

It's a beautiful golden Sunday afternoon in Remuera. Hands held around a circle – everyone gathered close on Ceal's white couch and kilim pillows and scattered wingback chairs. Today they're hoping Sananda might speak to them in voices through his channel, Ceal. Chanting helps to level out the energies of the group, turn them into one more powerful receptor. They start by humming softly, and as their voices rise, Harold's face contorts and Violet starts to tremble. The energy leaves his body with a moan and enters hers. The chanting brings Eileen progressively to new plateaux of bliss and consciousness. Her mouth goes slack and twisted as she marks them with her mind. Betty's happy just to be a part of something, not to be alone.

Because the group now has five new members, Thomas reads out a press release he's written, "based on the teachings of Mrs. Davis." He believes the larger world should be alerted to the possibility of disaster. He'll read it out, and then everybody in the room can sign:

New Zealand, 21 December: A terrible dawn breaks.
The Tasman Sea rises. Buildings on the fault line
tumble. The earth shakes. The flood moves north.

Thus far, the five new converts have gone along with

everything. But now a Q&A ensues. Why that date, and why New Zealand? Does that mean everyone will die?

Not if they shelter in the hills, he says. That's why it's essential to believe.

And then Eileen drops the final bomb:
"Of course," she says, "not everyone will have to hide."
"This is not yet for the press," Thomas leans in, whispering to his followers, "But some of us will be called to leave in Spaceships."

AND THEN, refreshments! Betty brings in a gorgeous silver flying saucer cake she's spent the last two days baking. Ooohs and ahhhs and everyone applauds.

Raeleen sneaks out to grab a smoke and Bob implores her to go back: This Can Save Your Life.

And then there's songs and party games, led by Betty. They play six rounds of a new game she's invented called *I'm Packing My Case for Space* until the list becomes so long that everyone keeps laughing.

Raeleen demands a private audience with the newly charismatic Dr. Armstrong. She tells her dreams, and Thomas stoically averts his gaze from Raeleen's bursting cleavage to give counsel. Susan plays some kindergarten songs on a guitar, it is a perfect day! And later, Ceal and Thomas lean longingly against each other on the stairs to talk about this marvel, while Violet instructs the group on the correct use of the Ouija Board. Ceal keeps everybody's glasses filled with orangeade.

Before the afternoon breaks up, Grace sits along with Ceal, her hidden tape recorder running.

"But it's all so extreme," Grace says. "Doesn't the gimmickry offend you?"

"If you want something badly enough," Ceal shrugs and sighs, "you want it to live for other people."

"But how do you know it's true?"

"When I write, my hands shake. The messages tear my thoughts away and it's like I'm outside space. There's no use wondering. You have to know it, in your body."

Ceal looks at Grace with a frightening degree of comprehension.

"So," she smiles. "Do you believe the teachings?"

And Grace turns her back on everything flip she meant to write and answers, "I believe in you."

SINCE THAT day on Vulcan Lane, Grace has been avoiding Gravity. On Monday she stays home to transcribe tapes of Ceal's meeting and make notes. She realizes Ceal's the catalyst for the group's extreme apocalyptic prophecies. Before Ceal entered, the ERG were a bunch of harmless crackpots who could've gone on studying other people's flying saucer sightings for another twenty years. And yet she senses Ceal's conflicted: that she's reaching after something deeper and more true than the absurdities she's preaching. Part of Grace wants to understand what Ceal knows. Another part already fully understands and is just wanting to protect her. Grace draws a little tulip beside Ceal's name on the sociogram she's making of the group and thinks: *I love Ceal.*

Around 4:30, Gravity knocks on Grace's front window. She's desperate to make up with Grace. She does this by avoiding any mention of the fight they had on Vulcan Lane. Grace tells her all about Ceal's meeting, and the way Grace talks about this woman makes her very queasy but she knows she'd better let it drop. Anyway Gravity is moving forward. She's figured out what's been depressing her is Lindsay, and yesterday she decided to move out of his place.

"It's too *abject,*" she confesses, hoping she can make Grace laugh. "All he talks about is the past and besides his stories don't add up. How could he've written the Situationist Manifesto with Guy Debord if he was living with Paul Bowles in Tangier?" What does Gravity want from all these men, Grace wonders. "I feel like a repository for hopeless bullshit. And besides, he calls me Dear."

Later when Gravity's gone home to whatever other junkie's flat she's staying at, Grace listens to the tape-recorded voice of Ceal:

> *The transcriber's work is to spread the news, tell a story and be fearless in the doing of it. Share what you have with one another. Share everything with those who hear…*

The transparency of Ceal's voice sends electric currents straight to Grace's heart. How could someone be so wrong, and be so right? And while she's swept away by Ceal's conviction, she also is afraid for her. She feels she's on the brink of something, like something's catching in her throat. She shuts back tears.

IN THE coming weeks, the ERG proselytizes with passion and conviction. They know that very little time remains.

At the Student Health Clinic at the University, Thomas no longer holds back from counseling his clients. Ceal spends her days waiting for new messages from Sananda and leafleting in Vulcan Lane. Even Betty at the hair salon has started warning customers to use acrylic tips instead of nail extensions. Nail extensions grow out with the nail over several weeks, and the world will not be here that long.

"They've set a date," Grace tells Gravity when they're walking up to Anthro class through Vulcan Lane. "They think I'm one of the new believers. It's like, the further out they push things, the more likely it will all come true. Because it has to."

Thomas has called an emergency meeting of the ERG tonight at Ceal's. Grace needs to tape the meeting but now she's terrified of being caught in this betrayal so she asks Gravity to come along.

Alright, says Gravity. Maybe they can make a deal. "What about the Hyatt, Grace? You going to come along with me?"

"I can't."

"What, afraid of lowering your density?" she sneers.

"Listen," Grace says, "the act was your idea and this is mine. I'm just trying to understand it."

UNIVERSITY FLOOD DOC FIRED, a billboard for the Auckland *Star* proclaims.

Grace is certain Ceal's in danger. "Oh Gravity, you have

to help me. Because don't you see," she says, "we're running out of time?"

BY 5 that evening, everybody knows that Thomas has been fired. Tonight there is no chanting. A nervous flutter passes around the room. Ceal has received no messages lately from Sananda. Perhaps her link is faltering? The consensus is, they'll wait together up at Ceal's until Sananda contacts them and tells them what to do. By 8 o'clock the room is littered with sleeping bags and empty packets of Doritos. Raeleen and Bob are ready to walk out, and this discord isn't helping, because the density must rise in order for Sananda to get through –

Arthur and Susan sit at Armstrong's feet like spaniel dogs or true believers. They want to get him reinstated at the university. Because, as Susan says, It's just not fair. Arthur says, "We'll pass round a petition."

Thomas recalls the martyrdom of saints. "No," he says, "You'll do nothing of the kind. It just confirms the teachings. I was clinging to that job. But now I'm ready. I put myself in Their Hands."

Raeleen, Harold, Lee and Bob are not so sure. They've brought along their backpacks just in case Sananda calls them. If they could they'd leave right now.

"He's a saint," Eileen gushes rapturously. "He's such an inspiration."

And then Betty just can't stand it anymore. Three weeks ago when she made that flying saucer cake, everybody'd been so happy and she'd been working for this, not just for Thomas but for Bob and Raeleen and Eileen and she'd made more sacrifices than any of them know, and yesterday that anorexic bitch receptionist told the boss how she was no longer doing nail extensions –

Betty leaps up from her chair. "Doesn't anybody care?" she shouts. "Today I got fired from the salon."

Thomas drops his head down to his knees. Ceal's face clouds up behind a nauseous wave of guilt.

The doorbell rings. She answers it. "Oh, Grace," she sighs, "You're here." There's a small pale punkish girl standing next to Grace. Ceal was not expecting a new person. "This is my friend Gravity." This gives Ceal a new idea.

"Gravity," she says, "I'd like to see you in the kitchen."

Gravity looks at Grace and swallows hard.

In the kitchen, Ceal backs Gravity up against the ice machine. "Tonight," she says, "we're going to get our orders from Sananda. It's been said that at the end, a stranger will appear."

Gravity's eyes open even wider.

"And you're here!"

Smiling, Ceal walks Gravity back inside. "Gravity," she tells the group, "will lead us."

Gravity thinks back fast to everything Grace has told her about the ERG, the tapes, the notes. "Let us – uhm – meditate," she says. Raeleen and Harold examine this girl skeptically. And why should it be her? But it's too late to dismiss any possibility and so reluctantly, they all join hands. Nothing happens. She looks to Ceal for guidance but Ceal is gazing somewhere at the ceiling. Gravity looks serious. "I think Ceal should say a few words."

Ceal masks profound annoyance with this girl as best she

can. "We are gathered here for a special reason," she announces magisterially. "The time is very close." She tips back her head in seance-mode. "We want our orders now, to leave the world."

The only answer is the humming of electric lights.

"Gravity? Is there anything you'd like to add?"

Gravity scrunches up her shoulders and shakes, No!

By now the group are only barely holding hands. Eileen is forlorn. Bob and Raeleen are disgusted. Even Thomas has no notion what to do. And then short stacatto sniffles rise out of armchair holding Betty, louder now, she gasps for air as Sananda's voice struggles to burst out of her –

"I've got the words! I've got the words! I've got the words!"

All eyes turn towards Betty as her enormous body spasms –

"I AM SANANDA! I've got the words, I've got the words! Sananda speaks! Oh no, it can't be ME… He says that, She who led you was good, but – oh, it can't be – Tonight, I bring you the greatest prophet – the Betty – that was, or ever will be."

And then the spirit vanishes, leaving Betty radiantly pleased.

"What about the orders?" Harold asks.

Susan sits at Betty's feet. "Ceal was wrong. They'll come from Betty."

"We have to get the orders."

Eileen is torn. "I don't know what it means."

"I can't describe what happened," Betty says. "But it was real. His voice rode over me."

Everyone but Ceal, who's in the kitchen summoning her

courage to call the whole thing off, gathers around Betty like Charcot's physicians. "Just let your mind go blank!" Thomas cries. "I'm trying," Betty says, and she knows that everybody's waiting and so she shuts her eyes again and says, "I Am Sananda." Twelve heads move closer, hardly breathing. Susan reaches for Betty's hand. "I bring you blessings now, and forever, and – forever and forever and forever –" Harold glares at Thomas Armstrong. "And forever, and forever, and forever." Thomas shakes his head, forlorn "And forever, and forever, and forever –" Susan turns away to Harold but Betty reaches for her hand – "and forever, and forever, and forever –

"and forever, and forever and forever" – Betty's desperate and pathetic litany echoes around the kitchen. Ceal paces, wishing she was never born. "And forever, and forever –"

And then Grace's face pops out at her from behind the kitchen door. Her expression is so trusting, so confident and strong that Ceal now knows what she has to do. She strides back into the room again, confident, in charge.

"It's alright," Ceal breezes. "I've had a message from Sananda. It's a confirmation. He says that I've been cleared. And when They come for us, I won't return again. And They're going to land at midnight, on the 21st of December."

"Where?" Gravity wants to know.

"On the tennis court. In my backyard."

December 21 – Sananda's Revelation

That morning Dr. Armstrong's press release finally ran in

in the New Zealand dailies as a gag, accompanied by a photo of Ceal's house, under the headline: *Flood Warnings in Remuera*. Eileen gave notice at her job, Bob sold his car. Moved by the group's willingness to withstand so much humiliation, Sananda's promised that the floods will not begin 'til 12:15, when everyone is safe aboard his spaceship.

Harold, until last week a metals engineer at the DSIR, has been researching the effects of interplanetary travel upon the human body. Metal heats up when passed through zones of heightened atmospheric density. In order to avoid surface burns, all metal objects must be removed from contact with the body.

At 11, everyone is dressed and ready for a party, excitedly removing steel-capped boots and gold and silver plated jewelry. "What about your bra?" Eileen whispers nervously to Grace. "Oh," Grace says, "it's velcro." The phone is ringing off the hook, reporters looking for a follow up. "No comment," Ceal blows them off. She's worried.

And then Marie Savage from next door rings the bell together with her bonehead boyfriend. The Savages have always hated Ceal and Edward. "Umm, Mrs. Davis?" Marie squeals. "We're having a little flood next door – in the toilet! Want to come over?" She and the boyfriend nudge and poke and nearly fall down laughing. Ceal slams the door. "My mum thinks you should be locked up," Marie hollers through the window. "You're fucking crazy!"

The clock on the mantel reads 11:52. Thomas rises solemnly. "I think it's time to go now."

The group file assemble in the dining room, beside the sliding glass doors out to the patio. "Okay," Thomas says, "let's practice the passwords. Ceal?" He and Ceal have been rehearsing this. Yesterday he begged her to reach Sananda one more time for special words, a confirmation they were truly chosen and he complied. Why doesn't Thomas call the whole thing off? That night when they were driving in their cars Ceal believed Thomas understood everything, and all she wanted was to be filled with spirit. Betty's nearly jumping up up and down, Eileen is in a tragic rapture, so Ceal throws her head back and intones –

"I Am The Porter."

"I Am My Own Porter," the group responds.

"I Am The Pointer."

"I Point My Own Direction."

And then the secret code, that Thomas made her use – "Where Is Your Hat?"

Twelve voices chant back solemnly: "I Left My Hat At Home."

Thomas slips his passport in his inside pocket. "And not a plan has gone astray," sighs Betty.

And they depart in solemn single file across the patio and march down lighted garden stairs onto Ceal's tennis court.

Crickets and a scattering of stars above the suburban halo of lighted streets and houses. And everyone fans out around the tennis court until they drift into a circle and then a song begins, without a leader –

> Who are we
> We are no one
> What do we want
> A human head
>
> Who are we

We are everyone
What do we want
A large field tent
and an airplane
and a large portable fan
Soooo We can go
Zoom golly golly golly
Zoom golly golly
Zoom golly golly golly
Zoom golly golly

God takes off like a jet!

And then the song trails off leaving nothing but the sound of crickets. Everyone is looking skywards through the darkness in between the stars but there are no meteors or spaceships.

Arthur never quit his job or gave up anything and now he's getting bored and feeling silly. He fiddles with his glasses. "My mother said she'd call the cops out if I wasn't home by 1."

Thomas grabs him by the shoulders. "Arthur, stop it, it's a test! They're doing this to us for a reason!"

But it's too late. Arthur's comment opens up the floodgates. It is the bitter end of expectation. "No!" screams Betty, sobbing, disappointment flooding through her body. "It's all lies! And I'm going to have to get another job, and I'm just out of beauty school and ohhhh, I can't cope, this is terrible."

Eileen's spent all her savings and Arthur's sold his car and as each person speaks their loss it dawns on them that Ceal still has her house and tennis court and car –

"She tricked us," Violet spits. Eileen and Bob rip up their idiotic passports, throw them at Ceal. Harold stalks off. Betty collapses onto Susan's shoulder, sobbing. Ceal cowers. She looks afraid and small. And Grace can't stand this. She doesn't want to study Ceal, she wants to save her.

Grace steps forward, shining like her long black hair and Chinese jacket, prepared to be a prophet.

"Wait," she says. "The world's still here!"

A curious expectant silence.

"You see – there isn't any flood!"

Gravity edges up to her, "That's bullshit."

But already Susan's half a step a head. "No," she says, a little bit incredulously, "She means *we* stopped it."

"We've been delivered?" Eileen asks.

And Harold picks it up: "We stopped the flood!"

"It's Christmas tidings and glad cheer!" Betty exclaims. Her tears are just a distant memory.

And everyone embraces, and someone starts to sing a traditional New Zealand drinking song, and everyone joins in, and Bob uncorks the bottle of champagne he'd brought along for Clarion and soon all of them are dancing.

> *Beneath the stars*
> *My ten guitars will play a song for you*
> *And if you're with the one you love*
> *This is what you do*
>
> *Dance, dance dance to my ten guitars*
> *Very soon you'll just know where you are*
> *With the eyes of love you'll see a thousand stars*
> *When you dance, dance dance to my ten guitars*

The lynch mob's turned into a kind of church school orgy. Ceal watches on, relieved. Grace is triumphant. She floats over to embrace a scowling Gravity, who can't accept that any people, even these, can be so easily satisfied.

"Grace," she says, "it's bullshit. It's sycophantic, sentimental bullshit."

She watches with disgust and shame as Eileen and Violet dance together in their floral printed dresses and Thomas waves his arms victoriously, and now the girls all start to dance a kindergarten finger-puppet game, Little Bunny Fou Fou.

"This whole town is bullshit! The entire country is bullshit!"

But are these people really very different from Lindsay and the other people that she knows? And why is it Grace can't see this?

"Oh fuck it girl," she says, stalks off, "I'm going to New York."

Grace turns and drapes her arm around Ceal Davis as the party rages on, twelve ecstatic people singing

Dance, dance dance to my ten guitars

Part 2: New York

YEARS PASS.

During Gravity's first months in New York City, the most impressive people that she met were artists and so she becomes one, too.

For seven years she stays entirely inside the city. She has no friends outside Manhattan and doesn't have the cash or confidence to be a tourist. Sometimes she rides the subway lines as far as they will go: Far Rockaway, Broad Channel, East New York and Coney Island, the Bronx Zoo. She walks alone, her bag stuffed full of books, a candy bar, an apple. She learns that every afternoon, the Bronx Zoo seals are fed at 3. Sometimes strangers talk to her. She takes this as a sign of magic. She walks along the Coney Island boardwalk sipping coffee, looking at the city's ancient artifacts of pleasure: the world's largest wooden roller coaster, the Hamburger Man, the rifle range. She is living in a double dream-world: the ghosts of other people's history she perceives in pieces of the urban landscape and the dreams that wake her up at night, sweating and in tears, of home. She looks at the Coney Island housing project and wonders if anybody knows which window that it was the singer Phil Ochs jumped from.

In some places outside Manhattan, the subway rises from the strip-lit tunnel darkness onto rickety tracks above the ground. It is here that Gravity believes she is really traveling. On the ride back home, Manhattan rises in the distance, queasy as a vision of the Emerald City through the poppies, before the train slips underground.

The longer that she stays here, the more impossible it gets to write a letter home. She is no longer who she was back in New Zealand and she doesn't really know who she is right now.

Dear Grace, she writes.

Great to hear about your new post. Keep me posted! Unfortunately, I don't sleep at night. My apartment's over a Chinese restaurant and the exhaust blows dead cat into my bedroom. It's a bit depressing going round to galleries with my slides all the time. Maybe I should come back –

She tears it up.

Dear Grace,
It's taken a long time to write back because I had so many thoughts. I was envious, not jealous, about your job. You have a chance to do something great. The Maori land thing is so important. You ask me what I'm doing –. There's no way you can compare it to public sculpture in New Zealand. I'm riveting metal bugs onto Coca Cola cans. I don't care if people like them. This is what I came to New York to do –

Does this sound too defensive? She tries again –

Dear Grace,
I know it's taken forever to write back. Things

are – okay. I was glad to hear about your new job.
Maybe you'll be Prime Minister by the time I get
home – though I don't know when that will be.
Last summer a good friend of mine died, and
I was in a group show at White Columns. I
bought a car. Your life seems like a fairy tale
to me.

This one will have to do.

1. Morning

Gravity's tiny bedroom is like a cabin on a ship. She's tossing in it, 9:10 a.m. She wants to shake this morning's dream out of her head, the branches of a kowhai tree are reaching out to her and then she watches her own arms being mangled by a train. The room's one barred window faces onto a narrow corridor of brick walls. The exhaust system from the Chinese restaurant down below, 16 inches from her bedroom window, roars.

2. Waiting for God

Gravity gives up sleeping and at 9:25 she makes herself a cup of coffee. She's listening to the Morning Program on the radio, WNCN. The strains of Beethoven's Sonata for Hammerclavier in B minor trail off into a string of weather bulletins and ads. It's 52 degrees in Manhattan. Who would know?

It's spoken in London. It's spoken in Tokyo.

It's also spoken in Paris, Berlin and Hong Kong. It's the universal language of business. Wherever your business takes you, Nordic Air speaks your language.

She pours some boiling water over coffee into a glass beaker.

That's why our Executive Class provides more business travelers with the most advanced comfort features available anywhere. Our personal limousine service brings you directly to the gate, to our personal arm-rest videos and fine gourmet dining.

Nordic Air. You'll find we speak your language.

Gravity knows she has to eat even though she doesn't want to. She takes a single mid-sized grapefruit from the fridge, cuts it in half and slices up the tiny sections.

The office hour is sponsored by the Puritan Bank of Manhattan – New York's oldest and most trusted financial institution.

The second room of Gravity's two-room apartment is a mess of boxes, drawings, shoes, her sculptures, a welding bench and unread magazines.

She presses hard to cut through the grapefruit's waxy surface. Something comes on the radio about religion, God –

Now here's a thought. Somebody told me
recently that they had reread a book after
many years, and that there was more in it
the second time. Now that isn't true –

A Japanese scroll hangs over the kitchen cabinet where the door should be. Its four characters mean, Great Hunger. It's a joke between Gravity and herself, the kind of joke she needs.

There wasn't more in the book than there
had been, the book was exactly the same.
Not one word had been added. But there
was more in them than there had been.
More experience, more insight, more
wisdom, a greater power to recognize
and appreciate.

I think of this when people tell me that the
Scriptures are 'irrelevant' – whatever that
means.

Maybe if there was more depth in the reader,
they would discover in the scriptures about
as much 'relevance' as they could bear.

I'm Maurice Boyd, Minister of the Fifth
Avenue Presbyterian Church, New York.

The time is now 9:40. Gravity sits at a tiny metal table beside the kitchen window, looking out into the airshaft. She is finding it very hard to eat that grapefruit. Swirls of Mozart mingle with the roar of the exhaust –

> *It's spoken in London. It's spoken in Tokyo.*
> *It's also spoken in Paris, Berlin, and Hong*
> *Kong. It's the universal language of business.*
> *It's spoken world wide, and wherever your*
> *business takes you, Nordic Air speaks your*
> *language.*

3. The Mail

It's 52 degrees in Manhattan. The sky, what she can see of it in the airshaft, is soupy gray. An ancient clothesline hung between her kitchen window and 2E hovers. She doesn't use it. Gravity comes back inside carrying her mail. Nothing but bills and notices for other people's shows. She checks last night's phone messages. Two.

> *Hi Gravity, it's Whitney Chase. I got your*
> *number from Jennifer Martin, the astrologer?*
> *She says you might be interested in a group*
> *I run. It's called, Chanting for Money. It's*
> *all women, mostly artists, and we meet at my*
> *loft in Brooklyn once a week. I can give you a*
> *really good price on the workshop. Call me.*
> *679-6082.*

Gravity ignores this. Now there's nothing left to do but work. She digs around for a drawing she made yesterday. Her bugs are turning into monsters. This one is a boll weevil with green and silver wings. She's fabricating these miscegenated insects in aluminum. She takes the drawing to the welding bench, puts her glasses on and studies it. Another message, from her friend Yvonne Shafir, plays on the machine:

> *A squirrel turning in its cage in a rotation of*
> *the celestial sphere. Extreme misery and*
> *extreme grandeur. It's when man sees himself*
> *as a squirrel turning round and round in a*
> *circular cage, that if he does not lie to himself,*
> *he is close to salvation.*

Gravity's wearing a bandanna, sweatpants and an old blue cardigan. At 28, she's still pretty, though her face is sharper than it was before.

> *Gravity, hope you're enjoying yourself. I'll speak*
> *to you soon.*

She lights her first cigarette of the day, squints and takes another drag. She isn't sure about these monster bugs. Still, she picks up a fresh sheet of aluminum and the metal cutters.

4. Factory Work

Gravity works for what feels like a long time. As she cuts and punches and rivets and drills she is no longer someone drowning in the loose ends of a morning. She is someone else – stronger and outside herself, absorbed in what she does.

5. Some Different Meanings of the Word Order

And then at 4, she leaves.

A chain-link fence surrounds the park that runs three blocks between A & B. Everyone is in their place – teenagers from the Projects shooting baskets in the court; nannies, children and the self-employed around the slides and swings; dogs and owners at the dog run. A pitbull races eagerly through autumn leaves.

Gravity's dressed up in her teaching clothes, hoping that her car will still be where she parked two days ago on Avenue B. Before she hits the corner of 10th and B, she bumps into her old friend-enemy Allan Jordan –

"Gravity," he says, and kisses her on the ear. "Allan," she says, "How are you?" Allan is a sleek young weasel and she's hoping he won't ask anything about her career.

"Terrible," Allan answers automatically. "You know my book, how I thought I had this total deal? Well it's coming out next month and they haven't budgeted a single penny to promote it. There've been no ads, no pre-pub reviews, nothing!" For a moment she is flattered he confides in her. "I mean Colin, what does he get?"

Gravity shrugs. She doesn't know.

"He gets a book tour. He gets an ad in the fucking *New York Times*. I mean we have the same fucking editor, Norah Reese. And everytime I see her all she can talk to me about is how successful Colin is. I mean, she pitches *me* to write a big fucking puff piece in the *Village Voice* about the New Gothic, in order to promote *him*. Argggh, it's not that I hate Colin, it's just he's lucky all this fang-de-siècle shit is selling."

Gravity thinks about the grammar class she'll be teaching in an hour in East Harlem.

"I mean, I just don't *know* about this. I've got a book coming out this month, I've got another book coming out in February –"

"Oh great," she says admiringly, remembering that Allan's semi-famous and he does write art reviews.

"I'm lecturing at Harvard –"

"Wonderful –"

"And Colin is on the *Voice* fucking A-list and I'm not making a penny! I mean, we know the same people, we have the same friends, we go to the same parties, what's wrong? And then Lynne tells me yesterday that his cousin owns *Grand Street*."

"The whole block?"

"No, the magazine. I mean, and *Grand Street* is Random House, which his uncle owns! And my family? They may as well come from fucking New Zealand! They don't even know what an artist does."

"Well, I – I read your last book and I thought it was great."

"Thanks," he shrugs. "So," I've been invited to give this lecture at Harvard, but it's just to the graduate association. I mean, when am I going to be able to live on my art? It's like I have this big reading at PS 1 that Willy is organizing, but they don't understand my work. It's like David and Martin. I mean, I was having dinner with David and Martin the other night, and I was telling them about this show I'm having at the Kitchen of my songs?"

The more he talks, the more she feels herself shrinking – "And – I thought that if I played up the Kitchen and PS 1 that they may be interested in doing – a book of my early journal writings – it's really just my coke ravings, but, uh

– They did say they wanted to do something for me and I don't want to give them anything good, you know? So I tell them that my career strategy is now to focus on my performance, and concentrate on my art, and David leans back, he looks at me and he says, 'Well? Is it working?' I mean, I ask you! Are these guys ever gonna support my work? No! They want me dead!"

4:30. Gravity wonders how traffic's moving on the FDR. "I've gotta go to class," she says. "I'm late."

One more down. He shrugs and grins. "Why is everybody going back to school?"

But there isn't any time left to respond to this and so she slouches off to find her car. "Dunno," she says. "I'll see ya." Just then a redhead in a bunny jacket and spike-heeled boots comes round the corner.

"Xandra!" Allan embraces her like she's just got back from a polar expedition, "You look beautiful." And is it really true, what Patrick said, that Xandra's NEA grant is being reinstated?

Xandra is ecstatic. She's truly blessed to get so much positive energy from her friends. "Oh, you know those old men in Washington, they had to give it back to me," she burbles. "And now that I've got it back, my career's going better than ever! I've booked out all these concert halls across the country, they're all sold out, I'm on all these talks shows, *Geraldo*, *Jenny Jones*. I couldn't have a better agent than Jesse Helms!"

Gravity gets into the passenger door of her 14 year old Plymouth. The driver's door was broken when she bought it.

Xandra knows that Allan is some kind of intellectual. "You know," she earnestly confides, "I really feel that I represent something. It feels good to be this political! I'm on a very important panel. It's called The Vagina and the American People. It's in Seattle."

TRAFFIC SLITHERS up the FDR like a caterpillar made of 100,000 metal pieces. Songs of the Crusades, a hundred thousand warriors traveling nowhere. Gravity is among them. A few live seagulls rise above the cars and office blocks and concrete bridges. What holds all of this together? The radio's tuned to WNCN, the stock reports,

and here is the business picture for today at closing the Dow was off more than 41 points at 3826.45 the 30 year US Treasury Bond fell 29/32nds pushing the yield up to 7.63 percent volume on the Big Board was heavy

A suspension bridge hangs over the plate glass river, pale light banging through the clouds far off in the northern sky above the Bronx.

471 advances, 1794 declines. The five most active Big Board stocks Syntex Corporation ex dividend up an eighth at 23 1/4 RJR Nabisco preferred C down an eighth at 6 3/8 RJR Nabisco down three eighths at 5 7/8 Philip Morris down 2 1/8 at 49 7/8 and Circus Circus Enterprises down 2 3/8 at 25 5/8...

Traffic is completely stalled. Gravity slumps behind the wheel.

The time is now 5 o'clock and coming up on the hour is World News sponsored by Trans Tech...

6. The Need For Roots

A Newport Sign above the gathering darkness at the Willis Avenue Bridge, "Alive With Pleasure." Traffic's finally moving.

Minutes later she's in strip-lit Room 204 at Touro College, pacing in front of sixteen Black American, Puerto Rican and immigrant Hispanic grown-ups in plasti-metal chairs. She is reviewing last week's lesson, What is a Sentence? "So every word," she rolls on, trying to make it new, "in every sentence is either part of the subject or the predicate." Already she's been doing this three years. "The subject tells us *what* or *who* we are talking about, so we underline it once." She waits for everyone to draw their lines inside their workbooks. "The predicate tells us what the who or it *does*, so we underline it twice." She wonders if they're getting it. "So we need a sentence. Somebody give me a sentence. Some words?" Tonight the room's unusually sullen. "We need some words."

No one responds. That asshole Allan made her 15 minutes late and most of them have kids and jobs. She knows they're angry. "Okay," she coaxes. "Let's start with a noun. What is a noun?"

"A person," a tall athletic Black woman says grudgingly.

Gravity smiles, remembering that the woman's name is Cynthia.

"Okay. Like Cynthia. Or a place, like Africa. Or a thing, like a car. Okay. We need a noun. Have you got another one, Cynthia?"

Cynthia glares. "Ma-ry."

"Good, okay," she says, writing on the board. "Mary is the

subject. A noun is at the center of the subject. The subject is at the root of the sentence. So without adjectives, Mary's just a simple subject, but that's okay, we'll keep it simple. Let's give her a predicate. What does Mary do?"

"She sings," says Isabelle Rivera, a stately woman of about 35 who is illiterate in Spanish, too.

"Mary sings," writes Gravity. "That's okay, but it's such a kindergarten sentence. I mean can't we say more?"

"What does she sing? Why does she sing?"

"A song," Charles ventures. He is husky youngish man in a shirt and tie. He looks like a car salesman.

Gravity knows they're fucking with her. Smiling dubiously, she writes the sentence on the board, then turns back to face these sixteen people squarely. "What kind of a song?"

"A good song," chirps Chiquita. Gravity knows Chiquita's slowness is for real and so she pushes her. "Good's no good, we want stronger words."

Cynthia's friend Rahina looks at Gravity in her shapeless linen skirt and cardigan contemptuously. "Mary sings a song about separation and disrespect," she riffs, mock-dubbing. "What she needs to sing is about unity in the community, about education, instead of separation." Slap, snap, high-five with Cynthia.

"Are you sure you don't want to transfer to Comp 3?" Gravity asks her quietly. "Absolutely not." "Okay," Gravity murmurs, and calls on Ruth, a church lady in the back.

"Mary sings a sad song." "Okay," Gravity writes, "and Raymond, why?" "Mmm... Cause she don't feel good?" Raymond offers sweetly. "Yeah, right, that's good. But – that's street English, and here we have to learn school English."

"Mary sings a sad song because she doesn't feel good,"

Carmela says. "Good, thank you, Carmela."Carmela smiles.

"And if Mary is the subject, what is the predicate?" The class is finally warming up. "Um, 'feel good'?" "That's part of it." "The rest!" Ruth's friend Yvette says confidently.

"Good, great, Yvette. See – I knew you knew it all along. Mary gets one line, the predicate gets two." She keeps on talking through it, drawing slashes underneath the sentence on the board, they finally have it, she turns to face the class triumphantly. "And why," she asks, "is this important?"

Silence. The class regards her curiously. And suddenly this question seems so large it's practically unanswerable. "It's important because if you can find the root of the sentence, the *heart* of the subject, everything else just falls around it and you won't get so lost –" Her eyes mist up, she swallows hard. "When you're reading."

Charles looks at her with something like compassion, and now she has to shift, get through the next two hours. "Okay, let's see what the book has to say about this. Turn to page 52, starting with Regina, who hasn't talked. Say the subject, then the predicate."

She's alright now, it's like it never happened.

7. Desperation

Alone again at home around 9:30 and wearing normal clothes, some jeans, a big white shirt, she puts some music on, turns the lights out, sits on the floor to read her Tarot. Her face is witchy in the light of five white candles. She shuffles to the backbeat of the tape, cuts and draws a card. She doesn't like the look of it, slips it back into the deck and shuffles. Cautiously, she draws again. Lays out the top three cards: the four of cups, the six of wands, the Fool. The fourth card's Death. She reaches for the phone and does what she doesn't want to do, calls Matthew.

"I'm fast asleep, so leave your message after the beep."

She hangs up fast and calls Fiona. "Hi, Fiona and Michael can't come to the phone right now –"

The tape shuts off. The couple up above are fighting, screams and wails and thuds. She puts a jacket on, goes out. Outside on Second Avenue the night's just getting started. Siren wails and streams of cars, drunken stockbrokers and people from New Jersey. She walks down Second Avenue through it all, past the dead ducks hanging in the window of the Chinese restaurant, like an explorer. Open eyes, round silver earrings and a cloche hat.

A motorcycle rips across her path on 9th Street. More sirens. She hears the strains of music drifting up the avenue, a live band playing in the street, guitars and violin, a conga drum, a female voice –

> Zoom golly golly golly
> Zoom golly golly
> Life takes off like a jet!

Is this the same song Grace and everyone were singing to Sananda in New Zealand all those years ago?

A crowd of younger people, different races, are standing round and listening to the female band. Gravity moves towards them.

> Family church school nation party
> Drown my dreams in tribal war

Family church school nation party
Build Berlin Walls shore to shore
Family church school nation party
Vainly beg their god to rest
Family church school nation party
Raise their flags upon my chest

The nighttime sidewalk's like a casbah, people selling their possessions, scarves and sweaters, clocks and answering machines, the orphan objects of the poor, spread out on dirty blankets. Gravity skirts past a tall man in an Army jacket counting out a roll of bills—

Who do I belong to
Soul or chromosome?
Boundaries and bloodshed
Earth seems so far from home

The lead singer is a woman in her late 40s, thin lips above a squarish jaw, deep eyes and creases in her forehead. Gravity wonders if she's looking at herself in 20 years and if so what this tells her. The other women in the band are younger.

When we were a rare animal
Newly human beasts of prey
It was one big God-hunt
We were free and easy
And we lived in skies of uncertainty
We were at large in time

The singer looks at Gravity as she passes. The Black man in the Army jacket and a short Korean haggle over the price of a wornout linen jacket. Three dollars, four. The conga drummer throws her head back like she's drowning in the rhythm.

What do I belong to
Soul or chromosome
Boundaries and bloodshed
Earth seems so far from home

On the other side of St. Mark's Place, at the Gem Spa, Gravity buys a magazine. When the light turns green she crosses.

A RED cursive neon sign hangs over Lucy's Bar on Avenue A. The jukebox roar pours out as she walks in. Maybe she'll run into some people that she knows here. Two girls in their late teens, early 20s, are playing a half-assed drunken game of pool. They're cracking up over some joke about a chicken's dick. They almost look like her and Grace. Gravity hasn't slept with anyone since last summer when she broke up with Matthew. That's got to change. Her back is a solid wall of loneliness.

Across the room, in one of the tall bar-stools sits an educated looking Black guy about her age. He's sipping a martini, reading. Boldly, she sits down next to him, catches the barman's eye and gestures towards the drink: "I'll have one of those, please." But when it's poured she chokes because she isn't used to drinking. The man looks up at her. "Bad day?" he smiles. It's as if he was just waiting for this to happen.

He radiates some kind of warmth that makes her not afraid and suddenly everything pours out of her – "No. It's just – I was stuck in traffic for two hours in the pissing rain, and I haven't had a show in nine months, and I'm sick of teaching English, and – It's just – have you ever had that feeling like, suddenly some things are one way and then all of a sudden it gets turned around and what seemed most wonderful suddenly turns out to be despicable?"

"Just because things seem serious, doesn't mean they really are," he says. "What's your name?"

"Gravity."

He gets the joke. He is the perfect guy. "Where's Grace?"

She can't believe this. "I don't know. I think she's in New Zealand."

"Sounds like the end of the world."

"No no, it's a real place."

And when he asks her what it's like, it seems he really wants to know, and so she answers –"Well, things in New Zealand have less weight. I mean, here in America, everything's so serious. But everyone is so alone." And then she gets embarrassed, takes her earring off and on, "I mean, I don't believe in nationalistic generalizations, I mean, what's what – this is just cocktail chat."

But the Perfect Guy looks straight through her awkwardness. "You don't talk like you're from there. You've worked on it. You've lost the accent."

'Well, I've been away." He waits, expecting more. "Well, I had to. But really – let's not repeat ourselves." She turns away.

"You're a very existential girl." She wonders if he's joking. "I mean, you've felt your destiny. You've embraced it. You're a romantic."

She laughs. "I'd like to be talking about books," she says, "but I haven't yet finished the book I'm reading. I mean, books are best!" She reaches for his book – *Horse Crazy* by Gary Indiana – but before she picks it up, he takes her hand.

"You know, this conversation is pretty great. Where'd you get such beautiful hands?"

She wishes against all better judgment that this is real, that she can trust him. Suddenly she's shy. "New Zealand."

"They're like squirrels."

"Yeah," she says, "and I saw squirrels in the park. I didn't think anything could live here."

"You know," he says, as if he's looking through her mind to what she needs to hear, "it's a little like how opinions change so fast. What's ignored or hated one year is celebrated the next. New York is like that. Things can turn around at any time. The trick is, to keep your own direction."

This makes her want to cry. He comforts her. "You seem really familiar. As if we met someplace a long time ago."

"Yeah," she says. Their hands are touching. She's visualizing everything. How his hands will move across her face and neck, and then she'll touch him. "So do you." And when they fuck their lips will touch but their hands won't move at all, as elegant as pears and coffee.

Two hours later she's alone again in her tiny cabin bedroom. Twisting round in bed, she can't allow herself to fall asleep, because she's afraid of dreams she half-remembers. Outside in her studio, the metal animals and insects around her workbench seem to come alive. They pulse and hum into her dreams until she hazily drifts off. It is a miracle.

THE NEXT morning she has an appointment at the New Museum at 10:30. She's dressed in standard artist black, black skirt, black tights, black sweater, a little makeup. This morning she does the coffee routine a little faster. Remembering that she has to eat, she slaps some strawberry jam onto a piece of matzoh. She takes a bite, then leaves it, carrying her black portfolio. There's nothing she can do about the thrift-store tan suede coat. Gravity is at that point in her career where people sometimes will agree to see her. That doesn't mean they like or want to help her. Still, she's moderately hopeful. Didn't William Burroughs write, "When all else fails, the final, the last resort, is a miracle?"

Gravity walks in the front door of the New Museum briskly.

The Senior Curator is a friend-enemy of Allan Jordan's, a monster in gold jewelry, designer sunglasses and a tight red suit. She appears to study Gravity's slides intently. "I see your work capitalizes on a commodifiable trope."

Is this a compliment? Does she mean the Coke cans? Gravity just says Thank you.

"I have a problem, though, with the metal. It's so contrary to the notion of the feminine unformed."

Gravity wonders how a soda can could ever be anything other than aluminum.

"After all, you're a woman."

"Yes?"

"And yet you haven't chosen to make an explicit

feminist critique the way most of your contemporaries do."

Gravity's confused. What do insects have to do with feminism? "Oh right," she says, "like Barbara Kruger's photos?"

"Exactly. You know, I see the sculptural medium as a serious problem in your work."

But Gravity never claimed to be a photographer.
"It's so – illustrational. You know, we're emphasizing criticality in this show." Gravity says nothing. "I see you're moving towards a kind of – expressiveness," she says disdainfully, "in the way you work with metal. But don't you think there's a fallacy in that paradigm? You position yourself outside the nature/culture dichotomy instead of trying to collapse it."

At this moment Gravity realizes the meeting isn't going very well.

"Face it hon, the East Village is dead. And anyway you're not making paintings. You know, I don't know why you paint the metal. Bright colors are never abject."

"What?"

"The problem is, you're neither abject nor sublime!"
"Sublime?"

"Yeah… Sublime. A beauty that transcends beauty. A phantasmic, non-realizable quality. You know, German, a little 19th century moonlight, Buchner, Bochner, Goya meets Hallmark!"

"But isn't that the opposite of abjection?"

"The sublime has always been on the side of shit. Face it, Gravity, your work just isn't shitty enough. It's illustrative of the peripheral conditions of shit."

"But my work is made out of garbage –"

The Curator starts to leaf through her unopened mail.

"Yes, but don't you think you need to distinguish between the mere debris of capitalism and a more heartfelt form of shit? More towards a manifestation of the transcendental sublime?" Her four-line console buzzes.

"Well, what are the dates of the show?" Gravity asks, as if this conversation isn't happening.

"Just give me thirty seconds, Martha," the Curator oozes to the phone. "Look, I'm sorry Gravity, but I really don't think we can accommodate you on this one." And then she offers some advice. "If I were you, I'd take another look at the kitchen." Does she mean the place where Allan Jordan is performing? "The kitchen. I think if you were to take another look at the kitchen, you'd find a deep source of new material you have not tapped into." And then, dismissing Gravity, she takes her glasses off, revealing a black eye. The Curator reminds Gravity of every curator she knows.

BACK ON the street before 11, Gravity walks down Broadway carrying her portfolio. She can't afford to let this meeting bring her down too much, and yet it does. She thinks she'll stop and see a friend who works at AIR on Mulberry.

When Gravity turns the corner off of Prince, the narrow canyon that is Mulberry Street begins to darken. White vapors swirl across the puzzle-piece of sky between the buildings. She stops and sees a blinding disc of whiteness moving towards her from behind the sky.

Could that disc of whiteness be Sananda's spaceship?

That Friday morning on Mulberry Street, Gravity is certain she's prepared to leave the world.

The film runs out. Black leader, music, credits.

Sources

Michael Adas, Prophets of rebellion – millenarian protest movements against the European colonial order, University of North Carolina Press, Chapel Hill: 1979

Georges Bataille, Le Bleu du Ciel, Jean-Jacques Pauvert, Paris:1957

Simone de Beauvoir, The Second Sex, translated by H.M. Parshley, Vintage Books, New York:1989

Jillian Becker, Hitler's Children: The Story of the Baader-Meinhof Gang, J.P. Lippincott Company, New York: 1977

Rudolph Bell: Holy Anorexia, University of Chicago Press, Chicago: 1985

Walter Benjamin: Hashish in Marseilles, in Reflections, translated by Edmund Jephcott, Harvest/Harcourt Brace Javanovich, New York: 1978

Hilde Bruch, The Golden Cage: The Enigma of Anorexia Nervosa, Harvard University Press, Cambridge:1978

Eva Buchmiller and Anna Koos, Squat Theater, Artist's Space, New York:1996 Meinhof's message from Andromedas written by Stephan Balint

Georg Buchner, Lenz in Complete Plays and Prose, translated by Carl Richard Mueller, Hill and Wang, New York: 1963

William S. Burroughs and Brion Gysin, The Third Mind, Random House, New York: 1977

A.H. Crisp, Anorexia Nervosa Let Me Be, Academic Press, London: 1980

Holland Cotter, Thek's Social Reliquaries in Art in America 78, no. 6 (June 1990) and Paul Thek's Time in Paul Thek The Wonderful World That Never Was, Witte de With, Center for Contemporary Art, Rotterdam: 1995

Philip K Dick: Valis, Vintage Books, New York: 1991

Marguerite Duras: Le Navire Night, Presses universitaires de Lille, Lille:1992

Leon Festinger: When Prophecy Fails; a social and psychological study of a modern group that predicted the destruction of the world, Harper and Row, New York: 1956

Simone Forti, Handbook in Motion, The Press of the Nova Scotia College of Art and Design, Halifax:1974

Fanny Howe: The Deep North, Sun and Moon Press, Los Angeles: 1988

Damien Hirst: No Sense of Absolute Corruption, interview with Stuart Morgan, Gagosian Gallery, New York: 1996

Aldous Huxley: The Doors of Perception, Harper & Row, New York: 1990

Mike Kelley, Death and Transfiguration, a letter from America in Paul Thek (Turin:Castello di Rivara, 1992)

Karl Marx, Collected Works, Volume 1, "Poems" translated by Alex Miller. International Publishers, New York: 1976

Ulrike Meinhof, Ecrits, translator unknown, Maison des Femmes, Paris: 1976 translation from French by Chris Kraus and Martin Baumgold

Thomas Nevins, Simone Weil: Portrait of a Self-Exiled Jew, University of North Carolina Press, Chapel Hill: 1991

Cherry O'Neill, Starving for Attention, Contiuum Publishing Company, New York:1982

Simone Petrement, Simone Weil, A Life, translated by Raymond Rosenthal, Schocken Books, New York: 1976

Rebecca Quaytman, The Notebooks of Paul Thek, in The Wonderful World that Never Was

Simone Weil, A Sketch for a Portrait, Southern Illinois University Press, Carbondale: 1966

Richard Rees, Brave Men, Gollancz, London: 1958

Avital Ronell, The Telephone Book, University of Nebraska Press, Lincoln:1989

Jean-Paul Sartre, The Emotions Outline of a Theory, translated by Bernard Frechtman, Philosophical Library, New York:1948

Paul Thek, The Wonderful World That Almost Was, Witte de With, Center for Contemporary Art, Rotterdam: 1995

Paul Theroux, Sir Vidia's Shadow, Houghton Mifflin, New York: 1998

Simone Weil, Gravity and Grace, translated by Arthur Wills, University of Nebraska Press, Lincoln: 1997
Simone Weil, Weil, Le Pesanteur et la grace, Editions Plon, Paris: 1947

Simone Weil, The Iliad or the Poem of Force, translated by Mary McCarthy with an introduction by Andre Weil, Chapel Hill Press: Philadelphia: 1957

SEMIOTEXT(E) NATIVE AGENTS SERIES
Chris Kraus, Editor

If You're a Girl Anne Rower	$7
The Origin of the Species Barbara Barg	$7
How I Became One of the Invisible David Rattray	$7
Not Me Eileen Myles	$7
Hannibal Lecter, My Father Kathy Acker	$7
Sick Burn Cut Deran Ludd	$7
The Madame Realism Complex Lynne Tillman	$7
Walking Through Clear Water in a Pool Painted Black Cookie Mueller	$7
The New Fuck You: Adventures In Lesbian Reading Eileen Myles & Liz Kotz, editors	$8
Reading Brooke Shields: The Garden of Failure Eldon Garnet	$8
I Love Dick Chris Kraus	$8
Airless Spaces Shulamith Firestone	$8
The Passionate Mistakes and Intricate Corruption of One Girl in America Michelle Tea	$8
No Aloha Deran Ludd	$8
Collapsing Dreams Luiz Bauz	$8
Aliens & Anorexia Chris Kraus	$8

SEMIOTEXT(E)
P.O. BOX 568, WILLIAMSBURG STATION
BROOKLYN, NEW YORK 11211
TEL/FAX 718–963–2603
www.semiotexte.org

Semiotext(e) Foreign Agents Series
Jim Fleming & Sylvère Lotringer, Editors

Semiotext(e) the Journal
Jim Fleming & Sylvère Lotringer, Editors

The Complete Smart Art Press Catalogue

Volume I (Nos. 1–10)

Voulme II (Nos. 11–20)

SMART ART PRESS
2525 MICHIGAN AVENUE, BUILDING C–1
SANTA MONICA, CALIFORNIA 90404
TEL 310–264–4678 FAX 310–264–4682
www.smartartpress.com